AMERICAN TREE HOUSES and PLAY HOUSES

Childhood Retreats from Yesteryear... Play Houses and Tree Houses of Today... and Six "Build-it-Yourself" Play House Plans

W9-CFC-399

Kathy Smith Anthenat

BETTERWAY PUBLICATIONS, INC.
WHITE HALL, VIRGINIA

Published by Betterway Publications, Inc.
P.O. Box 219
Crozet, VA 22932
(804) 823-5661

Cover design by Rick Britton
Cover photographs courtesy of (left) Minnesota Historical Society
and (right) Montana Historical Society
Photographs by Bruce A. Anthenat and Kathy Smith Anthenat
Typography by Park Lane Associates

Library of Congress Cataloging-in-Publication Data

Anthenat, Kathy Smith
         American tree houses & play houses : childhood retreats from
     yesteryear-- play houses and tree houses of today-- and six "build
     -it-yourself" play house plans / Kathy Smith Anthenat.
             p. cm.
         Includes index.
         ISBN 1-55870-204-0 (paperback) : $14.95
         1. Tree houses--United States. 2. Playhouses, Children's.
     3. Tree houses--Designs and plans. 4. Playhouses, Children's-
     -Designs and plans. I. Title. II. Title: American tree houses and
     play houses.
     TH4890.A58 1991
     690'.89--dc20   91-17995
                                                               CIP

Printed in the United States of America
0 9 8 7 6 5 4 3 2 1

June 15, 1992

Happy 8th Birthday, Sean! Since you are such a big boy now we thought you might like to design your own tree house. This book should help.

To two much-loved patriarchs:
Ralph Robert Smith
and
Samuel Hindenburg

and for one much-loved son, Sean.

Contents

About This Book

American Tree Houses and Play Houses was written to provide a permanent record of some of the fascinating varieties of childhood retreats built in the United States in past years, and to help generate ideas for families today who are thinking about building play houses for their children.

Part I includes a collection of old photographs and childhood memories about play houses, from the quilt draped over kitchen chairs as an indoor tent to the tree houses that have been built on the lawn of the White House.

Part II presents in-depth articles on fifteen selected play houses of the past. Whenever possible the children for whom the structure was originally created were interviewed. Various historical societies and museum personnel have also contributed information about these structures.

Part III contains more than one hundred photographs of current play houses. These are grouped into three classifications: those built at ground level, those built on stilts or atop a storage shed, and those built in trees. Browsing through all the different styles should help the reader decide what he or she does and does not like before constructing a play house in the back yard for the children.

Part IV supplies plans for six different play houses — indoor and outdoor, stationary and portable, elaborate and easy. These plans are only starting points; it is what you add to them that will make your play house a source of personal pride, whether it is the color scheme, the landscaping, the added tire swings, or other features.

I have spoken with numerous children to find out what made the difference between a nice play house and a well-used play house. Whether or not the children were allowed to participate in the construction was the biggest factor. Kids want to be involved in the planning and the building. Their involvement can range from small things like deciding exactly where to hang the tire swing to larger jobs such as digging holes for support posts or nailing on shingles. In one case, the father had built a tree house for his son—probably while thinking about that special one he had built as a child. After it was completed, the young son removed much of the lumber and rebuilt it—to his own specifications.

Anticipation is at least half the fun of any endeavor. Let the children flip through these pages and point out what they like the most—and what they don't like. Eventually, practicalities such as time, space, and money will have to be dealt with, but for a while let the imaginations soar.

PART 1

Play Houses and Tree Houses Remembered

Browsing through the Memories

Rummaging through an adult's bag of childhood memories can reveal some delightful mental souvenirs: going to the doughnut shop with Grampa on Saturday mornings; being chased by a feisty turkey on the way to the outhouse; getting a turn at cranking the ice cream freezer; making chains out of stick gum wrappers and sailboats out of walnut shells and toothpicks. And often, in the midst of the baubles and jewels, there is a play house.

Play houses are mini-kingdoms for children, bits of private space where adults are generally wise enough not to intrude unless invited. They nourish imaginations and give the child the chance to set the rules and standards. In the privacy of a play house a preschooler can practice the art of being a gracious host to two or three favored dolls and perhaps a well-mannered teddy or two. Many jars of "delicious" weeds have been canned in them on long summer afternoons. Older children use these retreats to read such classics as "Superman" and "Casper the Friendly Ghost," or to get acquainted with Miss Havisham, Trixie Belden, Elsie Dinsmore, and Huck Finn.

The construction of tree houses and play houses encourages camaraderie and innovation as pulleys are devised to lift supplies into treetop hideaways, and passwords are given out to The Chosen Few. Plans are made and executed to procure pieces of chocolate cake from the kitchen for the club members without getting caught and being sentenced to chores. We savor the experiences as a child and the memories as an adult.

A play house doesn't have to be fancy or expensive to earn a special spot in a person's memories. Monty Hall, television producer and actor, recalls the play houses of his childhood. "We children used to improvise, mostly with logs of wood, old used cartons, and any old tarpaulin that we could get our hands on; and from all this we fashioned our little hideaway house. We always had the feeling that when we crept into this little shelter, we were far from the world of reality. Of course, when our mother called us home for dinner we left our private world, took twenty steps, and we were home again."

The walls of Zella E.'s play houses were invisible. "When I was little we often just drew lines on the ground to mark out rooms and used scraps of broken dishes for china."

Jim S. used materials found in nearby woods for his boyhood play houses. "Several times I made a kind of lean-to on the side of a steep hill with some sticks and branches covered over with leaves. Those were good for about thirty minutes of relaxing and admiring my work and making a bed of leaves before it was time to go home, or back to Grandad's, or to do something else."

Imagination is the key ingredient in the construction of childhood retreats. A child can transform an old blanket and two kitchen chairs into a delightful indoor tent. Linda H. remembers the elaborate caves and tunnels she and her siblings would construct on the screened-in porch at the rear of their house.

"We would pick out the thickest quilt from the pile that Mom would allow us to use and drape it over the canning table to make a really dark main cave. Then we would use chairs from the kitchen to support the blanket tunnels that led to our side caves. We made those from a draped card table and two draped TV trays." The entire encyclopedia set from the living room would be used as weights here and there to keep the sagging blanket tunnels attached to the caves.

A quilt play house with a dozen or so stuffed animals, one little girl, and plenty of room to spare.

The windows of this cardboard play house were lined with masking tape to prevent paper cuts on small fingers.

Many play houses have been constructed of cardboard — both factory-made and kid-made. Bruce A. remembers the large shipping boxes for washers and dryers at his great-grandfather's appliance store in the early 1960s. These heavy-duty cardboard boxes came with a door, windows, and shutters preprinted on them with red ink. A dashed line near the bottom of the box indicated where to cut so that the play house could be lifted off intact for the lucky child of the customer.

Twenty years later, his son's first play house was made from two large boxes scavenged from a furniture store. Small windows and a toddler-size door were cut out of the larger box. The smaller box was then torn apart at the seams and fashioned into a gable-style roof, complete with felt marker shingles. That year during the Christmas season, in addition to the large Christmas tree in the living room, there was a smaller one for the play house.

Phyllis Schlafly, author and lawyer, has fond memories of her cardboard play house. "When I was seven years old, I had a cardboard play house that was approximately 5 feet square and 5 or 6 feet high. It was large enough for me to go inside and play with my doll. I loved it dearly."

For many children there wasn't just one special play house. Robert S. recalls numerous ones that he had while growing up on a farm in southern Illinois. His father once bought an old bus and converted the frame into a hay wagon. Robert and his younger brother and sister turned the discarded bus body into a play house.

In the wintertime the trio would pile up a huge mound of snow, as huge as child-sized patience and muscles allowed. Next, they poured water over the top of the mound, forming a hard, frozen, outer crust. Finally the snow underneath was carefully scooped out to form a glistening, frozen play house.

Another of Robert's play houses involved a large stack of baled hay. "We took some hay bales off the top, removed some bales from the center of the stack to make a cavity, and then carefully arranged some bales back on top to make a ceiling," he says. "Then we decided to enlarge it with a tunnel system. We would bust a bale and dig it out—feeding it to the cows so Dad wouldn't find out what we were doing—then bust another bale and dig it out."

Things were going along pretty well until their father used up enough of the hay feeding the cows that he got down to their handiwork.

One year Robert decided to build a tree house. He picked out a tree, gathered up scraps of lumber lying around the farm, some nails, and a hammer, and went to work. It turned out pretty well, so he decided to add a second story. Then a third.

"By this time the weight of all that lumber was making the tree sway back and forth pretty good whenever I climbed up in it," he recalls with a smile. "Dad evidently thought it was getting too dangerous because one day he took a chain saw out and sawed down the whole tree."

For some children, the tree by itself forms the perfect play spot. There was a lovely old weeping willow tree in the back yard of the home where Susan W. grew up. In the summertime the branches were green and full and touching the ground, forming a natural curtain on the perimeter of the tree. The cool, shady, secluded area inside provided a delightful setting for afternoon tea parties with her dolls, best friend, and the dog—if it would allow itself to be dressed in clothes befitting a lady's tea party.

Tree house perches have long been a favorite of children. When there is a strong breeze, the tree sways gently to and fro beneath them as they ponder the mysteries of the world and devise ways to escape the indescribably excruciating chore that awaits them down on terra firma. It is a place for meditation and relaxation, and — if parents' fears and the bogey man have been conquered—for overnight sleepouts.

The simplest tree house is made from a couple of 2 x 4s, a piece of plywood donated

This hollowed tree forms a private spot to sit and think. Courtesy of Minnesota Historical Society; photo by Guy Baltuff.

Two young ladies having a tea party in a small clearing inside two spruce trees.

by a nice old man down the street, a few nails, and a bit of skin from the knuckles. Some tree house builders nail short pieces of wood to the trunk of the tree for a ladder (amateurs soon learn that a minimum of two spaced out nails per board is required if you don't want them to twirl when you try to step on them); others prefer to shimmy up the tree or to climb up a knotted rope. The more difficult the access method, the more likely the success in keeping out undesirables such as younger siblings and grownups.

A finished tree house is a rarity. Generally, they are added to and improved upon until the opposite sex and/or cars are discovered. Sometimes a garden hose water supply and extension cord power are added. A hammock is a nice touch. A cooler and a little table would be convenient. By now things are getting a bit crowded, so work begins on a second story.

Educator and author Leo Buscaglia reminisces about the tree house of his past. "It was a group effort—built among the branches of a tree in a deserted area outside of Los Angeles (over forty-five years ago) that we called 'Bird Eye'. There was a small water drainage system that we dammed up to form a small lake under the tree. From our play house, overlooking our boy-made lake, we could see forever. What great secrets we shared there. Memories grew on branches like ripe fruit. Today the city has devoured Bird Eye—the stream, the lake, and the tree/play house. The memories are as alive as ever."

Lawrence W. Wetherby, former governor of Kentucky, did not have a tree house as a child but still remembers the one his son built in a large maple tree on their lot in Kentucky. It was made out of old boards and used a quilt for outside walls.

Sam Walton, founder of Wal-Mart Stores, Inc., understands about kids and trees. "I suspect it's just the nature of kids in their maturing stage to spend some time in trees, either in a tree house or sitting on a limb, dreaming and planning their future. I vividly remember the times our children played in that cherry tree in the front yard and how much they enjoyed that experience, even though it resulted in some broken bones. The bones mended and healed, and somehow the four children reached adulthood."

George Wallace, former governor of Alabama, writes that in his mind he can still see the various play houses that he constructed during his childhood. "We built tree houses in one big oak tree in front of our house where we spent one night. After that my father wouldn't let us spend any more nights there. He was afraid that we would fall out."

He also built "ranch houses." "We kids always went to the ten cent movie on Saturday to see pictures starring Tom Tyler, Hoot Gibson, and other cowboy actors; so we built ranch houses. We would make beds on top of one another like the camp houses of the cowboys. We built several of these. We would build one, and then we would decide on a different plan for the next one and build it.

"So, myself and the next door neighbor, Terrell Douglas Rush, made many ranch houses, and a lot of the other kids always came and played with us in them. We also named the ranch houses, such as the Flying X Ranch, etc."

Composer Ross Finney remembers the two play houses he had as a child. "The first was at the top of a tree in Valley City, North Dakota, from which I could view the entire domain in which I played. I could see the Indian Mound on the side of the hill; I could see the high bridge that crossed the valley; I could see the town dump where I collected valuable items; and I could see the shed where an old fellow was building an airplane that never flew. This was in 1912.

"When we moved to Minneapolis I had a play house in a nook in the attic. But from there I could see nothing. I could, however, surround myself with the books and gadgets I had collected and treasured. These hours were my own. My parents and brothers didn't intrude."

Fathers and grandfathers have been known to invest hours of labor into a dream-

A corner of a barn loft often becomes a play house for farm children.

come-true play house for a child. Former First Lady Nancy Reagan cherished the beautiful wooden play house in Galesburg, Illinois that her grandfather made for her. She will never forget "the many warm and wonderful times" she spent playing there.

Even state governors and United States presidents have catered to this traditional ingredient in childhoods. Caroline Kennedy had a tree house on the White House lawn while her father was president, as did Amy Carter during Jimmy Carter's term as president (see page 55). During President Benjamin Harrison's term his grandson, affectionately known as Baby McKee, had a tent play house at the summer White House at Cape May, New Jersey.

Albert B. Chandler, former governor of Kentucky, recalls, "We had numerous play houses at the Governor's Mansion when I was governor because we had numerous little children around. They really made the most of it, because they really had fun."

Dakota, the son of Governor Buddy Roemer of Louisiana, has a tree house of his own. It is complete with a pulley to get up and down with.

Located at the Governor's Residence in Tennessee is a large play house with two levels of play area: an enclosed ground level for the safe enjoyment of smaller children and a more open level about 8 feet above the ground. It is 12 feet square and was built in 1982 for the four children of Governor Lamar Alexander.

The first family to occupy Wyoming's Historic Governor's Mansion following its completion in 1904 were Governor and Mrs. Bryant B. Brooks and their five children. (Note: This mansion is now a museum.) Melissa Brooks Spurlock, the youngest of the four daughters, once recalled to the present curator of the museum that she and her siblings would stage plays under the eaves of the third floor, using the elevated area created by the ceiling of the portico for a stage. Neighborhood children joined them as actors in the plays, which the children wrote and cos-

tumed themselves. After rehearsals they would put on a performance for Governor and Mrs. Brooks.

In 1917 Governor and Mrs. Frank Houx and their four children moved into this mansion. During their two-year stay, the children used the red brick carriage house behind the mansion to stage circuses. Children at governors' mansions around the United States have similarly confiscated attics and carriage houses for play and pretense.

Terrace Hill, the mansion now serving as the Iowa Governor's Residence, was built in 1869 as a family home. The second owner of this estate, Grover Hubbell, had the ice house adjoining the carriage house converted into a play house in 1922 for his youngest daughter. The 16 by 16-foot brick building with four large windows and an arched door made a spacious clubhouse for Mary Beth Hubbell and her friends.

"We enjoyed it for three years before we lost interest due to growing up," she recalls. It was furnished with leftover chairs, tables, rugs, and lamps.

Research into other mansions occasionally turns up bits and pieces about play houses and tree houses. As a little boy, Bingham Powell often went with his mother to visit his grandfather, Judge George Greenwood Bingham, at the Deepwood Estate in Salem, Oregon. He recalled a tree house that his grandfather built him (most likely in the early 1920s) in the ancient yew tree that once stood near the back door. The family cook would sometimes relay his lunch to him via a line between the tree and the kitchen window.

Old photographs sometimes include interesting tree houses and play houses. These were gathering places for neighborhood kids, a place to play Andy-Over, Leap Frog, or Red Rover. While adults decorated the family home at Christmas time, the children often cut a small evergreen from a fencerow to adorn the play house. Buckbrush berries would be strung for decorations.

In urban areas, children often pressed a large culvert into service as a play house,

Caroline Kennedy's White House tree house was visible from the Oval Office so Dad could keep an eye on her. 1963 photo of Caroline, John-John, nurse Maude Shaw, President Kennedy, and "Red" Fay's daughter. Courtesy of John F. Kennedy Library and Museum, Boston, Massachusetts.

Benjamin Harrison McKee, age two, and his play tent at the Summer White House at Cape May, New Jersey, c. 1889. Courtesy of the Benjamin Harrison Home, Indianapolis, Indiana.

Historic Governor's Mansion in Wyoming, 1917. Light came in from the round window in the center of the pediment of the portico for the children's plays. Courtesy of Wyoming State Archives, Museums, and Historical Department.

equipping it with fruit crate chairs and a cardboard box table. Used cable spools have been turned into play houses by removing a couple of slats from the core for a door and cutting a small square on the opposite side for a window. A doubledecker play house could be made by bolting two cable spools together.

Some kids prefer to dig down for their secret retreats, as did broadcaster Eric Sevareid and Perdue Farms executive Franklin Perdue. "I never had a tree house," writes Mr. Perdue, "but two of my neighboring friends and I built an underground cave, which we covered and used as a little meeting/hiding place when I was probably around ten. No Huck Finn adventures, however."

Mail order catalogs, department stores, and toy stores have offered parents a variety of manufactured play houses. Many of these have survived one childhood and have been kept to be enjoyed by the next generation. The tree house that Eileen Ford, modeling agency executive, bought thirty years ago at FAO Schwarz when her son, Bill, was about seven is still being kept in the family.

"It is now in Washington, DC, but our two oldest grandsons have outgrown it and it is now going back to New Jersey for our two youngest grandsons who will start using it in a few years," she writes. "It matches our daughter's play house, which is still with us."

Both structures are white with green roofs and trim. The play house will soon be refurbished for the benefit of her young granddaughter, Alessandra. "I have always kept them painted with new roofs or ladders or whatever they needed, and hopefully one of the grandchildren will want it for their children, because they do not make them anymore."

When her son now browses through his bag of childhood memories, he finds that green and white tree house that made him the envy of the neighborhood and provided a place to escape from parents and governesses. Another person opens his or her bag and finds the special play house where . . .

Picnic Party at Cushman Park, c. 1884. Notice the tree house in the background. Courtesy of Nebraska State Historical Society.

People seated in a tree house, c. 1905. Courtesy of Minnesota Historical Society.

Women and children in a tree house built in a windswept spruce, probably at the Oregon coast. Courtesy of Oregon Historical Society, #0323G042.

Beautifully detailed play house but pretty grim expressions on some of the faces. Courtesy of Mississippi Department of Archives and History.

1932 photo of a child's play house and wading pool. Courtesy of Minnesota Historical Society.

Personalized play house with dutch doors in Winter Park, Florida, c. 1964. Courtesy of Judy M. Sweets.

David and Albert Marshall in front of a shack they built in a Portland, Oregon back yard, c. 1932. Earl A. & C.L. Marshall photo, Oregon Historical Society, #LOT311-1113.

Tiger "Athletic Club," St. Paul. Courtesy of Minnesota Historical Society.

Piano crate used as a play house by Kimball girls and their friends, Butte, Montana. Courtesy of Montana Historical Society.

Play house from a 1966 JCPenney catalog. Courtesy of JCPenney Co.

Play tower featured in a 1966 JCPenney catalog. Courtesy of JCPenney Co.

The 1975 JCPenney Christmas catalog included these two play structures. Courtesy of JCPenney Co.

PART II

Past Childhood Retreats

KNOLE COTTAGE

Knole Cottage is located in a clearing in the woods at Oakland University, about twenty-five miles north of Detroit, Michigan. Courtesy of Meadow Brook Hall, Oakland University, Rochester, Michigan.

The living room was the only room in the play house tall enough for Mr. Wilson to stand fully erect in. Courtesy of Meadow Brook Hall, Oakland University, Rochester, Michigan.

When this $22,000 brick play house was built for twelve-year-old Frances Dodge in 1926, newspapers called it "the finest playhouse in the world." It is approximately 22 feet by 30 feet, contains six rooms, and is scaled to approximately two-thirds normal size.

Frances was the daughter of Matilda and John Dodge. After John's death, Matilda was remarried to Alfred Wilson. Together they had this special child-sized house built to give Frances a place "to learn the fine art of homemaking." No expense was spared. Even the paneling and woodwork in the cottage match the quality used in building the magnificent 100-room, Tudor-style family mansion—Meadow Brook Hall.

Knole Cottage had the distinction of being the first all-electric home in the Detroit area. When it was completed, Frances christened it Hilltop Lodge because of its original hilltop location. She renamed it Knole Cottage on February 13, 1930, when it was moved to its present location on the estate to make room for other building projects. The name came from Knole Park, a country estate in England.

The living room ceiling is 7 feet, 3 inches high; all other ceilings are 6 feet, 3 inches high. Doorways are 5 feet, 4 inches high. An outside cellar door leads to a full basement, where the original electric heating system has been replaced by an oil system, and a water softener has been added. Small-sized bricks were used for the exterior, and bullseye glass was used in the front and rear doors. All of the wallpaper in Knole Cottage replicates the original style; replacements were chosen to match the original paper as closely as possible.

In the entry hall an ornate mirror hangs above a wrought iron table (a glass top replaces the original marble top that was broken years ago). There are pewter wall lamps with hand-painted shades, a fireplace matchholder that serves as an umbrella holder, and even a coat closet. Above the bedroom hallway is a pull-down staircase leading to a

cedar-paneled attic. Miscellaneous furniture items were stored up there, including lawn furniture for Frances' dolls.

The living room features oak paneling, a fireplace, and a window seat with five dainty windows. Among the furnishings in this room are a wing chair, a dropleaf maple table, and a maple secretary. The throw rug was handwoven in Newfoundland. A grandmother clock with 19th century works in a 1926 case still works, chiming "Give Us This Day Our Daily Bread." The face of the clock has the numerals 5 through 8 in reversed position, a common feature on very old clocks. The Oryhophonic Victrola, an early phonograph, is still in working order.

All appliances in the kitchen are childsized. Frances used the oven of the two-burner electric stove to bake cakes and cookies for her tea parties with friends. The original icebox was later replaced with a white counterheight refrigerator. A built-in ironing board folds out from the wall. In the kitchen bookcase is a collection of cooking pamphlets, which Frances ordered by mail from food companies. Wall cabinets hold a collection of Frances' china tea sets, glass baking dishes, tiny milk bottles, a square angel food cake pan, and more. There is also a child's cupboard with a rolltop and a porcelain worktop.

Furnishings in the dining room include a half-size maple harvest table with matching bamboo-turned chairs, and a china closet containing bone china cups and saucers, pressed glass, etc. A Chinese-style plant holder stands in the corner behind a three-panel silk screen. A tea wagon once used there is now stored in the attic.

In Frances' bedroom are pink curtains and bedspread with a flower trim. The white dressing table, youth bed, and matching chair have cane inserts. A glassfront cupboard holds a shoe collection and on the top sits a sewing machine.

The tile bathroom contains a small bathtub, washstand, and toilet—not to scale, but the smallest available in 1926. It is complete with monogrammed linens.

Frances' dream-come-true play house bedroom. Courtesy of Meadow Brook Hall, Oakland University, Rochester, Michigan.

The cottage even has a nursery for Frances' dolls. The pink and white furniture there holds the dolls' handmade dresses, fine hats, and a fur-trimmed coat. There is a matching swing and swinging cradle set, a musical chair, and a beautiful rug that depicts the story of Red Riding Hood.

A special building was also constructed for Frances' younger brother, Danny. A log cabin with a big fireplace, a work bench, and plenty of space to work served as a tool shop for him.

Even after Frances outgrew the cherished play house, her mother had the cottage kept heated and cleaned. The Wilsons eventually gave the Meadow Brook estate to Michigan State University for the establishment of another campus. In 1970, three years after her mother's death, the future of Knole Cottage was uncertain, so Frances Dodge Van Lennep had all of the furnishings removed from the play house and put in storage for safekeeping. She died the following year. In 1972 her husband and two children returned the furnishings to the cottage on loan so that others could enjoy the little house in the woods. With the help of a Girl Scout Troop, the cottage was restored to its original splendor and opened for its first public viewing on April 23, 1972. For more information about tours of the cottage, call or write:

Meadow Brook Hall, Oakland University
Rochester, MI 48609-4401
(313) 370-3140

Frances kept a guest book for the cottage. One entry reads simply: "Much is expected from those to whom much is given."

(Researched by Meadow Brook Hall Archives, May 29, 1990)

CHILDREN'S COTTAGE

The Children's Cottage is located in Newport, Rhode Island. Courtesy of The Preservation Society of Newport County, Newport, Rhode Island.

The Children's Cottage was built in 1886 for the seven children of Cornelius Vanderbilt at the family estate, The Breakers. The family home was subsequently destroyed by fire (1892), but the play house remains.

The Queen Anne Revival style of the exterior features half-timbering in the roof gables, small paned windows, and ornamental woodwork. The open front porch faces the Atlantic Ocean; the four carved wooden posts supporting the porch roof represent Drama, Greed, Music, and Vanity—characters from Dutch folklore, which were very appropriate as the Vanderbilts were from Holland.

The entire play house is approximately 35 feet by 24 feet. Ceilings are 7 feet, 6 inches high, and doors are 6 feet, 8 inches high. The play house has been restored to its original colors of gray, yellow, and rust.

The living room features a bay window and a large inglenook fireplace of Italian brick with two built-in seats. The children could pass firewood through a small window at the side of the fireplace. A large kitchen is equipped with a built-in stove, a sink, and a china cupboard containing dishes with the name of the youngest daughter, Gladys, on them.

VAN HOESEN PLAY HOUSE

1880s photo of the Van Hoesen play house. Standing at the gate is Rilla Van Hoesen (later Mrs. James Milbank Challis). Lucy Van Hoesen (later Mrs. Sheffield Ingals) is standing on the porch. Courtesy of Elizabeth M. Watkins Community Museum, Lawrence, Kansas.

This beautifully detailed little play house has had a special place in the hearts of several generations of young girls. It was built in 1878 by Isaac Newton Van Hoesen of Lawrence, Kansas, for his two daughters, Rilla and Lucy. The home of this Lawrence mayor was located at 323 Illinois Street, and the little cottage was listed by the post office as 325 Illinois Street.

It was approximately 10 feet by 10 feet, featuring a proportionately small front porch, a soldered tin roof, gingerbread trim, and shuttered windows that could be latched open or closed. Both the front and back doors had white porcelain knobs and key locks. An elegant chimney served the wood- and coal-burning stove sitting in a corner of the living room, near the back door. Isaac Van Hoesen and his older daughter, Rilla, made a trip to Marshall Field in Chicago to select furnishings for the play house.

By 1900 the Van Hoesen children had married and moved to Atchison, the father had died, and the mother also moved away. In 1901 Eli Wilson, a widower from Midland, Kansas, rented the Van Hoesen property and eventually bought it. He had five daughters who would bring the play house back to life again: Katheryne, Lilian, Alberta, and twins Hazel and Helen.

The next owner was Max Wilhelmi, who bought it as a Christmas present for his twin daughters, Ilse and Irma. The date the play house was moved to the Wilhelmi residence at 603 Ohio Street isn't known exactly, but it was probably before 1905. There were three other daughters in the family who also used it: Henelia (Nellie), Alwine, and Alice.

A decorating firm, Keith's of Kansas City, was hired to refurbish the play house. It was several months before it was ready for the Wilhelmi daughters to use. The exterior was painted white with green trim, and the interior was unpainted, varnished wood. White ruffled curtains were hung with heavy grocery store string.

The girls were able to cook on a cast-iron cook stove, which had a warming shelf, an oven, and another door in front for stoking firewood cut to length. Cooking equipment included iron pots, frying pans, stew kettles, lids, a blue enameled coffee pot, a small copper kettle for making tea, and wooden cooking utensils. A child-sized corner cupboard and a glass-fronted china cabinet held silver-plated flatware, white floral-design china, and etched red glass party dishes.

In a corner near the front door was a Morris reclining chair with soft, wide cushions. There was also a small oval dining table with spindle-back chairs. A swivel stool sat beside a scaled-down upright piano. In the bedroom was a red velvet one-arm couch, a dresser, and a rocking chair.

At least one more generation of Wilhelmis had the opportunity to use this play house before the property was sold to Dr. and Mrs. Philip A. Godwin in 1964. In the summer of 1975, the Godwins wanted to build a garage on the play house site and donated the play house to the Elizabeth M. Watkins Community Museum in Lawrence.

Architecture students from the University of Kansas disassembled it after careful drawings and photographs were made. "The play house had been built in a combination of the Eastlake and Stick styles of the latter half of the 19th century," says Curtis Bessinger, Professor of Architecture at the university. "However, the 'sticks' which were applied to the exterior were not only decorative. They were the structure that tied together the vertically applied tongue and groove boards of the single-board walls. The tongue and groove boards were the finish of the interior walls. The details of construction of the building had been very carefully thought out."

At the time of the dismantling, the play house was sitting partially on top of what had been a fish pond. By December of 1976 the reconstruction of the play house on the third floor of the Watkins Museum was completed. It is now painted beige with light brown trim. The original tin roof had deteriorated so badly that it could not be salvaged, so the wooden boards that were once underneath the tin now make up the roof. To show the condition of the play house before restoration, one section of peeling paint and weathered wood can be seen through protective plexiglass at the lower left of the front door.

Visitors can walk through the cottage on floors that have been carpeted to absorb sound. The original wood floor can still be seen in one closed-off room containing doll furniture.

HARRIET JANE CARNES' PLAY HOUSE

1934 or '35 photo of Harriet Jane Carnes sitting on the porch of her play house. Tied to a little tree is her pony, Sparky. Courtesy of Harriet Carnes Bonner.

In the early 1930s Grover and Bertie Carnes decided to build a play house for their only child, Harriet, behind their home in DeWitt, Arkansas.

"I think the idea of a play house began much more simply," relates a grownup Harriet, "but as is often the case, the idea grew once the project was begun."

The charming result was a 12 foot by 12 foot cottage made from cypress wood. It featured a wood shingled roof, a front porch with pillars, flower boxes beneath the windows, and decorative trellises. The interior was divided into: a 6 foot by 12 foot living room, a 6 foot by 6 foot kitchen, and a 6 foot by 6 foot bedroom. A screened porch in the rear ran the entire width of the house.

Several different craftsmen were employed to tend to specific details of the construction. Mr. L. L. Anderson, a woodworker from DeWitt, made the little doors and windows to scale and sawed the siding to a narrower size than for a regular house. A brick mason from Little Rock built the chimney and half-moon front steps.

The play house was wired for electricity. The living room walls were papered with muted striped blue, pink, and white moiré, and at one end of this room was a working fireplace, complete with miniature andirons. A small-scale upholstered mauve sofa and chair and a matching bed and dresser set were made by the Rhodes, a father and son who operated a furniture and upholstery shop in Stuttgart, Arkansas. The bedroom wallpaper was pale green. Ruffled priscilla curtains hung on the windows—blue in the living room and green in the bedroom. There were also window shades, which are still in the house and working.

The kitchen contained a pale apple-green dinette table and chair, tea cart, counter space, and built-to-scale wall and base kitchen cabinets, which held dishes and cooking utensils. Above the wainscoting were original Mickey and Minnie Mouse figures on pale yellow fabric.

In 1979, three years after her mother's death, Harriet Carnes Bonner decided to donate the little play house and all of the remaining original furnishings to the Arkansas Post County Museum near Gillett, Arkansas. The structure was moved to the museum, where Mrs. Myrtle Bergschneider and her husband, Ralph, went to work to restore it to pristine condition. Since then literally thousands of children have come to visit this delightful child's retreat.

VILLA LAURETTA

Laura Maddox standing on the brick porch of Villa Lauretta in 1924. Courtesy of Laura Maddox Smith.

Few play houses match the elegance of Villa Lauretta, a play house built in 1924 in Atlanta, Georgia. It was constructed at Woodhaven, the family estate of Mr. and Mrs. Robert F. Maddox, for their seven-year-old daughter, Laura. An Elizabethan style of architecture was used in the design of both Woodhaven and Villa Lauretta.

A winding brick path led to the timber and plaster structure, which had a red-tiled gable roof and two windows on each of the four sides. Beneath each window was a flower box planted with flowers and hanging vines. Among Laura's housekeeping chores were keeping the walk swept and watering the flowers.

The little home was complete with electricity and running water. Soft, neutral tint rugs covered highly polished wood floors. In the center of the house was a hallway with 18th century gray wallpaper, a painted console table with a hanging mirror, and a flowered hooked rug. A bowl of sweet peas and wrought iron stands with ivy sat on the table.

The first room on the left side of the hallway was the living room. Flowered, glazed chintz was used in the decorating scheme — for the upholstered winged chair, for the valance above the lettuce green draperies, and for the center of a round pillow on the parchment-colored chaise lounge. A spinet desk held stationery embossed with "Villa Lauretta." Two hanging walnut bookcases were filled with books for Laura to read. This room also contained a rocking chair, an antique foot stool from New Orleans, a tilt top table, a shaded lamp, a mahogany wall clock, and a parchment and green painted Victrola in working order.

Behind the living room was the bedroom where Laura would nap. A parchment-colored, blue-piped bedspread covered the blue four-poster bed. The rose-pink organdy ruffled curtains were edged with blue ribbon and tied back with little pink and blue bouquets. Lamps with pink ruffled shades sat on the three-mirrored dressing table, along with silver toilet articles and rose-pink bottles of perfume. There was also a blue and ivory sewing stand, a little desk, two pink and blue hooked rugs, and an assortment of Laura's dolls.

The dining room was the first room on the right side of the hallway. All of the furniture in this room was hand-painted a soft blue-green using the design of the chintz draperies: a drop-leaf table with six chairs, a sideboard containing small size silver flatware and embroidered linen, a china cupboard containing a pretty flowered china set with tea cups and saucers, and a tea cart. A pair of end tables with mirrors above them stood on each side of the hall doorway.

Behind the dining room was an immaculate, white-tiled kitchen. Built-in cupboards were filled with dishes, cooking utensils, glass baking dishes, pans, coffee pot, silver teapot, egg beater, waffle iron, etc. An electric stove allowed Laura to try out her cooking skills. In a corner was a sink for cleaning up afterwards. She could browse through cookie recipes at the porcelain table.

Laura invited her parents and a few friends for lunch on the day she held her housewarming. Many tea parties followed. Years later Laura's daughter also had the opportunity to play in this exquisite little cottage.

Eventually, Laura Maddox Smith gave the contents of her cherished little house to a friend who was building a play house for her daughter. The play house was removed in the 1960s when the estate was prepared for the present Georgia Governor's Mansion.

Seven-year-old Laura Maddox in her beautifully furnished play house bedroom, June 1924.
Courtesy of Laura Maddox Smith.

THE LITTLE HOUSE

On a bronze plaque beside the front door of the Little House is written "For every child who looks through my windows or walks through my rooms, and especially for those who do not have to stoop to enter."

The beautiful child-size house located behind the Ellwood Mansion in DeKalb, Illinois, probably holds the record for being moved the most number of times of any large play house in the United States — at least ten times. This two-story play house was built in 1891, most likely at North First and Fisk Streets, almost directly across the street from its current location. It was scheduled to appear in a trade fair parade to commemorate the opening of the Leonard-Atkinson Shoe Company factory.

After appearing in the parade, the Little House was bought by Mr. William Ellwood for his daughters, Jean and Elise. William was the oldest son of Isaac L. Ellwood, who amassed a fortune manufacturing barbed wire and built the Ellwood Mansion in 1879. The play house was subsequently moved to the southwest corner of First and Augusta.

It was moved again to the home of Mary Ellwood Lewis at 335 College Avenue for her daughter, Louise. Mary was one of Isaac Ellwood's daughters.

It was soon returned to the Ellwood estate, near the spot where it now sits, so that Perry Ellwood's daughter, Patty, could play in it in the 1910s. Isaac had died and Perry had inherited the mansion.

In 1922 it became part of a miniature farmstead exhibit for a Farm Bureau anniversary meeting. It had the distinction of being the only real building in the exhibit; the rest were only painted, built-to-scale fronts.

There were various other homes through the years. The Burt Oderkirk family purchased it for their daughters, Lila, Ida, and Ellen. For nearly forty years it stood in their apple orchard and delighted generations of neighborhood children who were invited there for tea parties and sleep-overs. In 1953 Ida Oderkirk operated a summertime nursery school in it.

Eventually Mrs. Oderkirk decided to return the Little House to the Ellwood Mansion, which had been turned into an historical museum. In the spring of 1973 a new foundation was constructed on the rear lawn of the Ellwood Mansion for it, and the Little House was moved once more. In 1986 it was restored to its original color scheme—yellow and tan—using paint scrapings and an old photograph as guides.

Thousands of children have come to visit this exquisite little play house, which has sat in so many different yards and brightened so many childhoods. Many adults do a double take when viewing the Little House from the steps of the mansion; so perfect are its details that unless there is a person near it for size comparison, you can't be certain whether you are seeing a miniature house close up, or a beautiful, old-fashioned, two-story house in the distance.

HOSFORD PLAY HOUSE

1919 or 1920 photo of Katherine, Eleanor, and Alice Hosford at the Hosford play house in Lawrence, Kansas. Courtesy of Alice Hosford Chapman.

This precious little play house was located behind the home of Mr. and Mrs. Clitus Blair Hosford at 1846 Barker Street, Lawrence, Kansas. Alice Hosford Chapman, the middle child in the family of five children, fondly remembers the part it played in her childhood.

"We had a beautiful fish pond in our back yard," she recalls, "and back behind it in the back lot, a darling little play house."

Her father obtained it from the home of Mr. Haskell, a prominent architect in Kansas. Clitus Hosford, a real estate man, noticed the little play house on the Haskell property on Haskell Avenue and asked Miss Haskell (the one unmarried daughter still living there) if it was for sale. After hearing that he was the father of four small girls she offered it to him, since no one else in her family expressed any interest in it. The little building was then moved to Barker Street, much to the delight of the daughters.

"I don't know exactly when the house was built or when it came to us," states Alice, "but it was pretty old when we got it." She was born in 1913 and the play house was acquired during her early years. She estimates that the Haskells had used it for at least fifty years before that; fortunately, it had been well maintained and was in excellent condition.

The 8 foot by 16 foot structure was painted a light gray with white gingerbread trim. It had four double-pane windows that slid up and down and a door that could be locked. The roof was shingled and there was a chimney, even though there was never a real stove inside. It was said to have been constructed mostly with screws rather than nails.

The interior was divided into two rooms, a dining room and a living room. The walls and cathedral ceilings of both rooms were finished with beautiful, dark walnut paneling. The dining room was often used by the children for picnics; it had a small plate rail all around the room above the door top ". . . on which we kept some demitasse cups and saucers (a gift of our aunt) until they all were broken!"

Another member of the family, Elizabeth, remembers the little walnut bed and dresser with a mirror that their father made for the play house. Any available small-sized chairs and tables also ended up in there. There was a small broom for their sporadic cleaning sessions.

The neighborhood was full of children, causing their mother to set down some guidelines for the play house. "Mother had to make a rule that only girls played in the house," says Elizabeth, "but the boys continued to hang around and tease and start fights so often that sometimes the house became more of a fort than a play house."

The children would play Andy-Over by the hour on the outside of the play house — throwing a ball up and over the roof to the team on the other side. Because their home was such a gathering place for the neighborhood children, Mrs. Hosford sometimes had to limit the playgrounds — boys in front and girls in back or vice versa.

"I am sure we had many 'club meetings' in the play house," says Alice, "and judging from some old ledgers saved from those days, which I saw a number of years ago, we must have organized and elected officers about every three days!"

Mainly she remembers the play house being used for housekeeping and caring for dolls — their children. "I remember it full of girls and dolls and doll carriages and tea sets and doll clothing. I remember vividly times when we pretended our dolls were ill and we had to send for the doctor, but I guess the doctor (if male) if he ever arrived was barred from entering the house."

The Hosford family eventually needed a bigger home and moved to one on Louisiana Street. Unfortunately, the new yard was too small to accommodate the children's beloved play house.

"It broke our hearts that we couldn't take it with us," recalls Alice.

The home behind their new home did have a similar play house (most likely the one now preserved at the Watkins Community Museum) but one of Alice's sisters, Eleanor, refused at the time to set foot inside it. Years later, when Alice asked her why, she explained, "It was simply because I was so MAD at our father for not moving our play house with us that I refused to be coaxed to play in the other one!" Eleanor was eight at the time.

The play house probably no longer exists, except in the memories of the children who played there. At one time it had been moved to a filling station at the corner of 23rd and Barker and was being used to store supplies such as oil cans. Later owners wanted to clear the lots for house sites, and the little play house was most likely destroyed.

TWINHEIM

Erna and Olga Carl were about four years old when this photo was taken of them and Twinheim, most likely in 1924. Courtesy of Elizabeth M. Watkins Community Museum, Lawrence, Kansas.

Around 1924 a play house was built at 721 Indiana Street in Lawrence, Kansas, for the Carl family twins, Erna and Olga. The name for the play house came from the German background of their mother, Elsa Barteldes Carl. "Heim" means home in German, so the play house was called Twinheim.

A grownup Erna Carl Gilliam estimates that the structure was approximately 8 feet by 10 feet, with an additional 4-foot porch on the front. The exterior was painted a cream color with blue trim. "It had a door, I think not quite full-sized, and four windows —one on each side—and a flower box on the south side that we always put flowers in. I think it was regular height. Adults could stand in it."

A year or so after the original structure was built, a smaller second room was added on the north side for a kitchen. The stove for the new kitchen was a replica of an old iron wood stove. The kitchen was also equipped with pots and pans, a pretty tea set, and child-sized table and chairs painted green.

Their mother made it a cozy little retreat with curtains on the windows and cushions on the wicker rocking chairs. Under the south window was a window seat with a pad to lie down on. Electricity was added later so that the children could play in the house in the evenings.

"At Christmastime we put up decorations — pine greenery and later lights across the porch and down the posts," says Erna.

Her sister, Olga Carl House, also fondly remembers Twinheim. "I recall having friends over and serving *very* sugary tea and munching cookies. Those were happy days."

ELLERSLIE

Jean and Clara Clemens sit on the front porch of Ellerslie. Courtesy of the Mark Twain Project, Bancroft Library, University of California, Berkeley, California.

The play house of the three daughters of American author Mark Twain (Samuel Langhorne Clemens) was located not at the family home in Hartford, Connecticut, but rather at Quarry Farm in Elmira, New York, where their aunt and uncle, Susan and Theodore Crane, lived. Aunt Sue was their mother's older sister and the Clemens family often summered at her home, arriving in the middle of June and spending about three and a half months at the relaxing hillside setting. Two of the Clemens children were born at Quarry Farm and the oldest daughter, Susy, was named for her aunt.

Aunt Sue had the board-and-batten play house constructed for Susy, Jean, and Clara in 1886. It was large enough to accommodate a crate for a stove, a table, chairs, shelves, and dishes. The children had been reading *Scottish Chiefs* by Jane Porter at the time and decided to name their new play house after the hero of the story's hermitage, "Glen of Ellerslie."

About a hundred yards from Ellerslie was a small octagonal building, which was constructed especially for Mark Twain in 1874 — also a gift from the generous Susan Crane. A winding path and stone steps led to the little cottage with eight large windows and a beautiful view of Elmira and the surrounding hills. In the quiet solitude of this study Mark Twain spent productive days working on *The Adventures of Tom Sawyer, The Adventures of Huckleberry Finn, The Prince and the Pauper, A Tramp Abroad, Life on the Mississippi*, and other stories.

In 1983 Quarry Farm was given to Elmira College and is now the site of The Center for Mark Twain Studies. The stone steps and foundation of Mark Twain's octagonal study remain, but the building was moved to the Elmira College campus in 1952. Ellerslie — the mini-estate where cats lounged while children played—no longer exists.

PLAY HOUSE OF EDWARD BRINGHURST III

Edward Bringhurst III outside his childhood play house at Rockwood. Courtesy of Rockwood Museum, Wilmington, Delaware.

Interior view of the converted play house. Courtesy of Rockwood Museum, Wilmington, Delaware.

Only one child ever grew up at the magnificent Rockwood estate in Wilmington, Delaware: Edward Bringhurst III. Edward was eight years old when his family moved there in 1892. His grandmother, Sarah Shipley Bringhurst, had given Rockwood to her son, Edward Bringhurst, Jr., and his wife, Anna.

The mansion was built by one of Edward's ancestors, Joseph Shipley, who moved into it in 1854. Between 1892 and 1893 a stone farm outbuilding with a slate roof was retrofitted to provide the child with a private spot of his own.

The converted play house would have made a wonderful hand-me-down play house for the next generation, but Edward never had any children. Eventually the play house rotted away, leaving only the foundation. The mansion itself is now a museum, open to the public since 1976.

AMY CARTER'S WHITE HOUSE TREE HOUSE

President Jimmy Carter enjoys a moment with daughter, Amy, and grandson, Jason, at the White House tree house. Courtesy of Jimmy Carter Library, Atlanta, Georgia.

When Amy Carter went to live in the White House, her father, President Jimmy Carter, saw to it that her childhood wasn't left behind. In his book, *Keeping Faith*, he writes, "After she and I designed a tree house and it was erected within the sprawling silver cedar on the edge of the south lawn, we really felt like a family at home."

Nine-year-old Amy had been using her platform-style tree house for a full week in the spring of 1977 before the press was told of its existence. She had even slept out there one night with a friend. The nursemaid who accompanied them reported to the press that the girls had spent a cozy night—armed with blankets and Cokes and cookies — but she was pretty cold out there under the night sky.

The rimmed platform was not actually attached to the tree; instead it sat about 5 feet off the ground on four posts. White House carpenters constructed it from leftover lumber, staining it to blend in with the tree. To reach the perch, Amy and her visitors had to climb along the sturdy branches of the tree.

Like so many children, Amy liked to bring books with her to read in her special place, but not every tree house has a view of the Washington Monument and Jefferson Memorial—and Secret Service men keeping a watchful eye for possible intruders. After the press reported that the child of our "no frills" president now had her own no-frills tree house, a lot of people wrote Amy to ask, "How do you build an Amy Carter play house?"

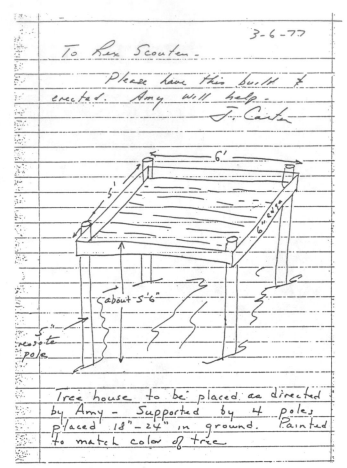

President Jimmy Carter's original sketch for Amy's tree house. Courtesy of Jimmy Carter Library, Atlanta, Georgia.

THE BRIARS PLAY HOUSE

The Briars play house is nestled among the trees at Bar Harbor, Maine.
Courtesy of Maine Historic Preservation Commission, Augusta, Maine.

Information about this play house is very scarce, and facts are hard to verify.

The cottage is located on an estate in Bar Harbor, Maine, where a mansion was built in 1881 for J. Montgomery Sears of Boston. The mansion was built on Shore Path, at the end of Wayman Lane, and was called The Briars. In 1909 Thomas Walsh bought The Briars for his daughter, Mrs. Edward McLean. In 1968 it was torn down, except for a servants' wing, which was converted into a guest house.

The background of The Briars play house (also sometimes called the McLean play house) is more difficult to determine. One account has the elaborate play house designed by Andrews, Jacques, and Rantoul of Boston, and built in 1898—presumably for J. Montgomery Sears' grandchildren. Another account says it might have been built as a studio for Sears in 1893. It has also been speculated that the play house was built by the McLeans in the early 1900s.

The play house is still privately owned and is somewhat obscured by vegetation.

Notice the beautiful windows on the side of The Briars play house. Courtesy of Maine Historic Preservation Commission, Augusta, Maine.

A PLAY HOUSE WITH NO DOORS

Lova Cline's play house sits solemnly beside the tombstone of the Cline family.

There is a cemetery in the little town of Arlington, Indiana, where you will see more than the usual headstones and flowers. On the north side, at the grave of a six-year-old girl named Lova, is a play house. The 5-foot high white building has six windows but no doors. It was built for an invalid girl who could play in it only with her eyes and mind.

Lova Cline was born in 1902. She was the daughter of George and Mary Cline of Cambridge, Indiana. From birth the little girl was afflicted with an illness that never allowed her to walk or even sit up. Although she spent her days lying in a bed, there was one thing that would put a sparkle in her eyes—a petite and beautiful play house built by her father. He was a bridge carpenter and put his skills to work to create this special gift for his only child.

The house had a tin gabled roof, poplar weatherboards, and considerable scrollwork. George Cline also made furniture for the play house, including a table with a little vase of flowers and four chairs. There were three dolls inside: one lying in a baby cradle, another sitting in a wheelchair made of wrought iron, and another standing in a corner. On a railing above a window were more vases.

On October 20, 1908, little Lova died. After she was buried at East Hill Cemetery, her father put the play house that had given her such pleasure—if only from a distance—on her grave. He and Mary never had any more children.

When Mary died in 1945, there was not enough room near her daughter's grave, so she was buried on the north side of the cemetery. Soon after, Lova—and the play house— were moved to her mother's plot.

It has been reported that George, grieving after his wife's death, suggested that the play house be destroyed. A caretaker pointed out to him that it had become a cherished memorial. The small building was then given a fresh coat of paint and a firmer foundation, and the caretaker's wife supplied it with new lace curtains and new rugs to replace those that mice had destroyed. The next year, at age seventy-nine, the father died and was buried beside his wife and daughter.

The little white play house has become an area landmark. Lova Wooten, an Arlington resident, has made a point of seeing to its upkeep. Her parents and the Clines had been good friends, and she was named after their daughter. During her childhood, the Clines often brought gifts for her when they came visiting.

Unfortunately, heartless thieves have repeatedly stolen the furnishings inside the play house. The original furniture made by Lova's father was stolen in 1959. Friends pitched in to refurnish the house with doll furniture. It was robbed again in 1981, and again it was refurnished with furniture, dolls, and even a new miniature wheelchair. In 1986 thieves broke in again. The replacement furniture this time is a scaled-down version that cannot be seen from a car.

In 1986 the caretaker of the cemetery took the play house to Tweedy Lumber in Carthage for the installation of aluminum siding (which unfortunately covered up the original scrollwork). During this time a new concrete foundation was poured for it at the gravesite. The lace curtains now hanging in the windows were made from an old tablecloth.

Visitors continue to drive by to see the play house with no doors, and think about a little girl who lived so briefly and the father who loved her so much.

Children stop to peek inside the play house with no doors.

MINIATURE RAILROAD DEPOT

An old photograph shows Locomotive No. 100 in front of the miniature railroad depot. Courtesy of Gordon Regan.

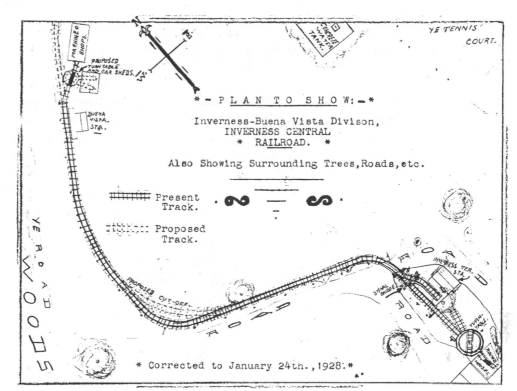

Sketch of the railroad line for Locomotive No. 100.
Courtesy of Carlie Cameron Collier.

In 1987 Leigh Anne Cameron and Amanda Cameron visit the miniature depot where their grandfather, Malcolm Graham Cameron, and his friends once waited to ride on the Inverness Central Railroad. Courtesy of Carlie Cameron Collier.

Saturday, May 23, 1927 was a day of fun and celebration at Inverness, the estate of Barton Haxall and Mary Randolph Cameron in Gordonsville, Virginia. It was the grand debut of the Inverness Central Railroad. This miniature railroad system was built for their only child, Malcolm Graham Cameron, who was fourteen or fifteen at the time. Invitations had been sent out with free tickets "good for any number of rides, Inverness to Buena Vista and back." The 15-inch gauge, steam-operated railroad included 260 feet of track.

The work that led up to that day began four years earlier when Locomotive No. 100 was bought from a junk shop. The little coal-fueled engine was 10 feet, 6 inches long, 3 feet high, and weighed 220 pounds. It was reported to have once been used in a ride open to the public at Forest Hill Park in Richmond.

The parents decided to wait until the engine was in good working order before beginning work on the track or buildings. For the first two years it wouldn't run at all. During the winter of 1924-25 the engine was completely overhauled and refitted. It was finally necessary to remove the whole boiler and clean the inside in order to get up steam, and trouble with the injector was overcome by installing a steam-fed water pump.

In May of 1925 grading for the track began, and one hundred feet of track were laid. Two-by-four pine ties were placed 24 inches apart, and 12-pound steel rails were spiked to them. Crushed white rock was used for ballast. Unfortunately, there was more trouble with the engine and no more track was laid that year.

In the spring of 1926 another 160 feet of track were laid for a total of 260 feet. The Inverness Terminal Station was built near one end of the track, along with a train shed and turntable. At the other end of the tracks was a smaller Buena Vista Station and shops. Neighborhood children were so eager for the train system to be completed that they enthusiastically joined in to help construct it.

Malcolm Graham Cameron put together a fifty-page scrapbook about the entire project. It includes layout sketches, snapshots, and commentary—starting from when the engine was bought and continuing beyond the opening day celebration. The photographs include wonderful details such as a mountain goat standing on the roof of the Buena Vista Station while workmen are sawing shingles off its crest. There are shots of the concrete ash pit, the ballast crushing plant, "the Section Gang" spiking down a rail, and a bad rail where a minor wreck occurred. The train included at least two open-top passenger cars, Cars 51 and 52.

In the years following the grand debut the little railroad kingdom expanded in size, but eventually Malcolm Graham Cameron outgrew the little depot and Locomotive No. 100. Legend has it that during World War II part of the tracks were donated for scrap metal drives.

Mr. Cameron sold Inverness Farm after Mrs. Cameron died, and around 1950 moved to Lancaster County, Virginia. Subsequent owners of the estate sold the little engine and removed what tracks remained to clear the way for a septic tank. Years of neglect have taken a toll on the miniature train depot, the only remaining part of the Inverness Central Railroad system. However, the current owner has taken an interest in the history of Inverness and hopes to restore the depot in the near future.

VIERHUS MINI LOG CABIN

Lou Marilyn Vierhus and her mini cabin in the woods. Courtesy of Montana Historical Society, Helena, Montana.

On a late summer day in 1937, Lou Marilyn Vierhus received a very special gift from the men of Camp Nine Mile, a Civilian Conservation Corps camp located on the slope of Squaw Peak, west of Missoula, Montana. The gift was a charming child-sized log cabin. The four-year-old girl was the only child at the camp where her father, Louis M. Vierhus, was superintendent.

Leader Paul Hendershot came up with the idea of building a play house for her, but soon a whole crew was in on the construction of it. Foreman Charles Engbretson and his group of fifteen men used their spare time in the evenings for a month to work on the cabin in secret. The anticipation of the look on the little girl's face when they would finally present it to her was one motivator, but Mr. Engbretson also believed the mini log cabin would be a good training project. Most of the men at the camp came from eastern Montana, and he believed the experience in log-building construction there might enable them to build their own log homes.

The structure was built at no cost to the government. The 4-inch diameter peeled logs used in it were unusable for other purposes. Shingles, paint, and floor lumber were donated by Foreman William Longpre. The finished play house was 6 feet by 6 feet on the inside, 8 feet high, and had a 2 foot by 6 foot front porch. There was a 20 inch by 50 inch front door and three 10 inch by 12 inch windows. The floor inside was varnished, and wood shingles—painted green—covered the roof.

Sometimes the children of friends of Louis and Marilyn Vierhus would come and play with Lou Marilyn in the mini cabin in the woods. Cupboards inside contained small cooking pans and dishes. There was a sink and a counter covered with red oilcloth. A flagstone path led from the play house to the Vierhus home, which was located just outside the CCC Camp.

Lou Marilyn played in her little log home until 1942, when her father joined the Army. When the war started, the CCC men were asked to enlist and Camp Nine Mile was closed. The Vierhus family moved to Seattle, Washington, until the war ended.

Marilyn Vierhus recalls the morning they left for Seattle. "Lou Marilyn got out a large piece of tablet paper and wrote 'Keep Out' and nailed it to the front door of her play house."

Afterward, the little cabin was moved to the nearby Nine Mile Remount Depot, a government-owned facility that supplied mules and horses to Forest Service crews for fighting fires and other uses. Children of various foremen at the facility through the years have had the pleasure of playing in Lou Marilyn's little log cabin.

PART III

Tree Houses and Play Houses Today

GROUND LEVEL PLAY HOUSES

Cardboard play house purchased from a department store Christmas catalog.

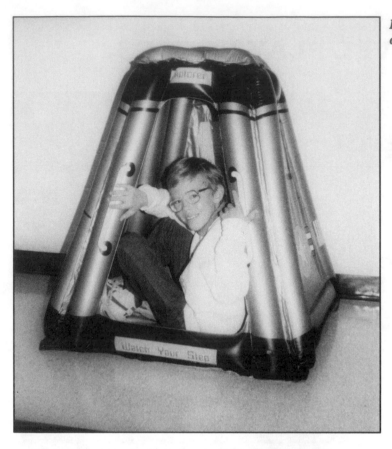

Inflatable play house for aspiring astronauts.

This little plastic play house with a half door and shutters fits nicely on a rear deck.

An inviting pot of red geraniums on the porch offsets the "KEEP OUT" notice written on the screen door of this kid-made play house.

A white and gray play house constructed from this, that, and the other thing.

Two-level play house tucked beneath a tree in a corner of the yard.

This simple design is approximately 4³/4 feet by 5 feet.

An upper deck provides additional playing space for active children.

White 4 foot by 5 foot play house with dark green trim and a patio block front porch.

This unusual A-frame play house has a balcony, porch, and painted-on flower designs.

This structure includes a bit of everything: tunnel, climbing net, etc. "He just started at one end and kept on going!" says the wife of the builder.

A beautifully landscaped, slightly elevated play house.

This pink play house with lavender trim has sloping sides and roof.

A plain white play house becomes something really special with the addition of some exterior decorations.

This play house has clean, simple lines, a concrete foundation, and concrete front steps.

The children who played here aren't children anymore, but the play house remains.

Only a few feet of sidewalk separate the front door of this play house and the back door of the family home.

This little red play house sits empty now at the back of the property, but it hasn't lost its charm.

The double 2 x 4 design used here catches the eye.

The once-long legs on this play house were cut short when the owner wanted to move it to a new house.

When this play house was built thirty-five years ago the fireplace was on the inside. The building was jacked up and moved off to the side later.

This small log cabin was assembled from a kit by Santa Claus on Christmas Eve by lamp light in the back yard. A ground squirrel sitting on the ledge of the back window is checking out the accommodations.

Landscape timbers were the building blocks for this 8 foot by 12 foot child-sized log cabin. A long wood walk extends from the family home to the cabin.

This small greenhouse has been converted into a clubhouse for the children. The reverse might also be a great recycling idea for old play houses.

Before being moved and converted into a play house, this structure was used for an office at a car dealership.

An old chicken house is given a thorough cleaning and put to use as a play house.

This wood-shingled building is actually used as a Santa's house in a town square, but wouldn't it make a beautiful play house in a wooded setting?

This former Santa's house was auctioned off and is now a play house.

A talented grandfather built this play house for his grandchildren. When the family bought a new home six miles away, the play house moved with them.

Another work of love from a grandfather. It is complete with wallpaper and a telephone, and has a bronze plaque beside the door which reads "Made special for Brooke - Bess - Becci - Brenna with much love, 1985 Grampa Steury."

It took about a year to build this elaborate windmill play house. It is 14 feet to the top of the dome and 21 feet to the top of the sails. The dome can be rotated to move the sails in the direction of the wind.

Inside the front door of the windmill play house is a small curving stairway leading to a cozy upper room.

This little structure was originally built as an attractive paper recycling deposit in a church parking lot, but it would also make a nice spot for prayers at a church day care center.

This train engine on wheels provides a cubby for relaxation and imagination.

This caboose play house is complete with bunk beds and seats so you can peer out of the upper windows.

A real caboose at a local park was the model for the carpenters to construct the $^5/_8$ths scale caboose play house.

Large and small gingerbread men trim this play house.

A father of six children built the brick play house on the left, which is a child-size version of the family home on the right.

This play house/school bus stop was built in a shed and then moved out to the road. It is approximately 8 feet by 6 feet inside, 9½ feet tall, and extends an additional 2 feet on each side for the railing. In the background is the family home.

"Simsville" is located in a grandfather's expansive back yard. Each of the street signs bears the name of one of the grandchildren.

One of the play houses in Simsville is a little red school house.

PLAY HOUSES ON STILTS

This plastic stilt play house has all the basics for the littlest tykes.

This play house takes its cue from the popular movie.

This A-frame play house on stilts is approximately 6 feet square, 6 feet high, and 6 feet off the ground. It includes a ladder, fireman's pole, and tire swing.

This roomy play house provides airy shade on hot summer days.

Access to this play house is by a rope ladder on the far end.

Children can go up the ladder, across the small balcony, and down the slide.

The stairway for this play house is built directly under it instead of off to the side. High sides and railings increase safety for little ones.

The peak of the roof extends out to accommodate swings.

This recycled play house has been moved from its original location for a new set of kids to enjoy.

The rear of this play house has a triangle window at the peak; underneath is the ever-popular sandbox.

Metal poles support this play house and two flights of stairs.

Part of an amusement park slide that was being dismantled is used in this play house for triple-sliding fun.

A dutch door is used in this play house located over a spacious sandbox.

Plans for this rustic style play house were drawn by an eight year old who wants to be an architect. His father built it.

A steep ramp provides access to this open roof play house.

This enclosed structure makes a dandy private clubhouse.

A ladder goes up through an opening in the floor of this sturdy play house.

A short, square opening is used for the entryway here. Lining the windows up in front and back allows the breeze to pass right through.

This platform play house needs no roof; the surrounding evergreens provide adequate shade.

A simple small roof provides a cozy, shady spot for the children, yet does not hide them from Mom's watchful eyes.

This canvas top play house and gym set was built from a kit.

This play tower is large enough for a whole birthday party full of kids. Notice the alternating triangle-shaped decks.

Located on the edge of the woods, this swing set includes a play house with wood sides and a canvas top.

Space age design play house is perched above the swing and slide set.

This petite play house set offers plenty of ways to exercise young bodies.

Grampa built this play house. The see-through sides provide safety and visibility.

This roofed play house doubles as one end of a clothesline.

The geometric designs here make for a pleasing addition to the back yard.

Children have a choice of a variety of play areas and levels in this structure.

Extensive use of latticework dresses up this interesting play structure.

When the owners of this back yard went away on vacation, Grampa went to work building this surprise for his grandchildren.

This elevated play house is attached to the rear patio deck.

Another eye-pleasing use of latticework.

Here is a great way to make the most of a beautiful view of a river. It won't be just the children who use the comfortable shaded swing underneath.

Decorated shutters add a charming touch to this play house. There is plenty of seating on the pair of benches below.

Stockade fencing is used for a play fort. A half wall was placed just inside the entrance for added privacy.

This old play fort once included a roof. Before building it, the father used matchsticks to make a scale model.

The old fort includes this interesting homemade seesaw.

A natural combination—little boys and high shady places. Below the play house is a small-sized lawn furniture set.

A windmill about to be demolished was relocated to this farm, and the sides and steps were added for an elevated play area.

This play house with an RV ladder was built first, and the storage shed added later.

This play house is attached to the side of the garage. The entire play area is neatly edged with landscape timbers.

Built beside a back yard pool, this structure has a play house on top and a storage area for pool equipment on the bottom.

Braces support the overhanging balcony of this play house.

This play house is built above a storage shed and features a charming upper porch with railing.

This pastel yellow play house/storage shed with white trim was built twenty-five years ago with plans ordered from a magazine. The father installed an intercom system between the play house and home.

A two-story structure with a regular door on top and a small garage-style door on the bottom.

The play house door on the upper level and the storage shed door on the lower level are on opposite sides of the building.

The lines of the vertical siding go well with the lines of the railing on this play house/storage shed combination. Landscape timbers are placed to make a ramp for getting the lawn mower into the shed.

TREE HOUSES

A 10 foot high tree stump elevates this 8 foot by 8 foot play house. The current occupants are a mother cat and a litter of new kittens.

Another stump play house with a minimum of roofing and plenty of room for stretching out and thinking.

The owners used a section of the trunk of a 100-year-old tree that had died for the base of this play house.

A triple-decker tree house.

This tree house—made of scavenged real estate signs—is almost hidden in a low area beside a road.

The little boy whose head is peeking out is responsible for the construction of this cozy tree house.

Latticework is used for the sides of this tree perch. Boards extend over to the other tree to provide extra support and a place to hang a swing.

Still a tree house, but closer to the ground than most.

Pieces of lumber are nailed to the tree to make a ladder for climbing up to the square access hole in the bottom of this tree house.

This tree house is still under construction, but two smiling faces are already trying it out. Trees support two corners of the 7 foot by 11 foot structure, and used telephone poles support the other two. The floor is approximately 10 feet off the ground. Conduit pipe is used to make the ladder.

Three-fourths of the platform is framed in as a play house, and the remaining one-fourth provides a small deck.

This closeup shows how the platform is built around the tree trunk.

This tree house has an extension cord power supply.

Most tree houses are built in maple or oak trees, but this one is nestled in an evergreen tree.

This tree house was assembled on the ground first and then hoisted up into the tree.

Four tree trunks grow up through this tree house. The holes where the trunks go through the roof were lined with rubber from inner tubes to allow the tree room to grow while keeping out the rain.

The boy who built this tree house was only eight when he started it.

Another spring, another new tree house under construction.

Two trees are used to support this play house.

This large tree house sits in the crotch of an old tree.

Steps and landing that lead up to a tree house are large enough for an adult.

Four trees are used to support this diamond-shaped platform for a soon-to-be-constructed tree house.

A closeup shows the open triangle in one end of the diamond-shaped platform where the access ladder is attached.

PART IV

Plans
for
Six Play Houses

COMBINATION LOG CABIN PLAYHOUSE/STORAGE SHED

Designed by Bruce A. Anthenat

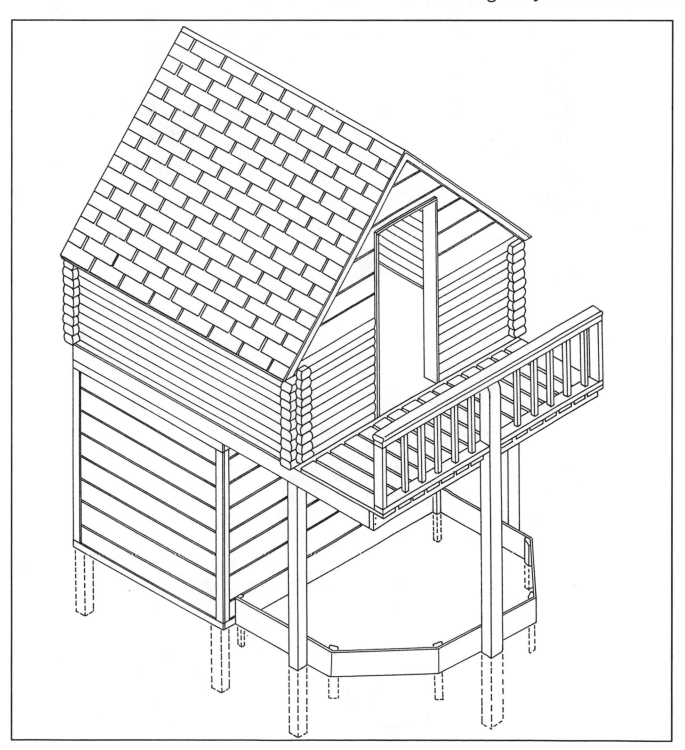

OPTIONAL STEPS WITH HANDRAIL

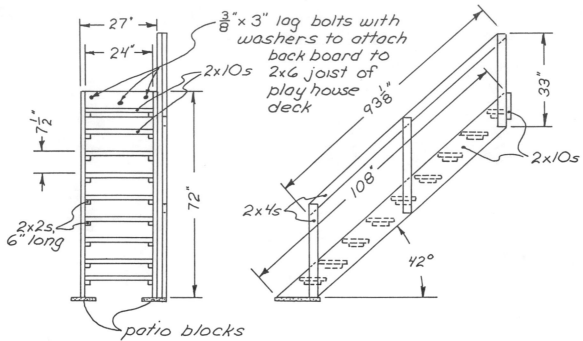

$\frac{3}{8}$" x 3" lag bolts with washers to attach back board to 2x6 joist of play house deck

27'

24"

2x10s

7$\frac{1}{2}$"

72"

2x2s, 6" long

patio blocks

93$\frac{1}{8}$"

108"

33"

2x10s

2x4s

42°

Use galvanized deck screws for assembly.

REQUIRED MATERIALS

treated 2x10s, 2 @ 10' long & 4 @ 6' long
treated 2 x 4s, 1 @ 10' long & 1 @ 8' long
treated 2x2s, 1 @ 10' long
3 - $\frac{3}{8}$" x 3" lag bolts with washers
4 concrete patio blocks
galvanized deck screws.

OPTIONAL FIREMAN POLE

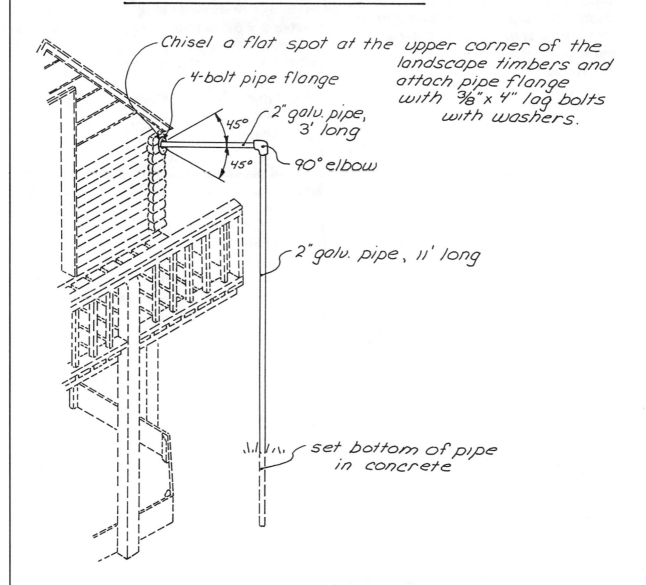

Chisel a flat spot at the upper corner of the landscape timbers and attach pipe flange with 3/8" x 4" lag bolts with washers.

4-bolt pipe flange

45°

45°

2" galv. pipe, 3' long

90° elbow

2" galv. pipe, 11' long

set bottom of pipe in concrete

REQUIRED MATERIALS

2" galvanized pipe, 3' long
2" galvanized pipe, 11' long
90° elbow for 2" pipe
Standard 4-bolt 2" pipe flange
concrete mix
4 - 3/8" x 4" lag bolts with washers

This play house uses landscape timbers to imitate a log cabin. Let the kids suggest additional features—a slide, rope, chain of tires, or fireman's pole — to make it uniquely theirs. Store your lawn mower and garden supplies conveniently in the shed underneath. Or eliminate the shed and make a shaded sandbox of the entire underneath area. Perhaps you will decide to add a baby swing there now and frame in the shed next year.

Required Materials

Treated 4 x 4 posts, 8' long	6
Treated 4 x 4 posts, 10' long	1
Landscape timbers, 8' long	42
Treated 2 x 6s, 8' long	4
Treated 2 x 6s, 10' long	2
Treated 1 x 12s, 10' long	2
Handrail, 8' long	1
1¼ x 6 deck planks, 8' long	7
2 x 4s, 8' long	12
2 x 4s, 6' long	17
Treated 2 x 4s, 8' long	7
½" CDX plywood	3 and ¼ sheets
¾" treated plywood	2 sheets
⅝" V-groove siding	6 sheets
1 x 3 trim, 8' long	16
Roof shingles	1 square
Concrete mix	6 bags

(Also required: concrete patio blocks, door hinges, deck screws; materials for ladder or fireman's pole, if adding)

SUPPORT POSTS LAYOUT

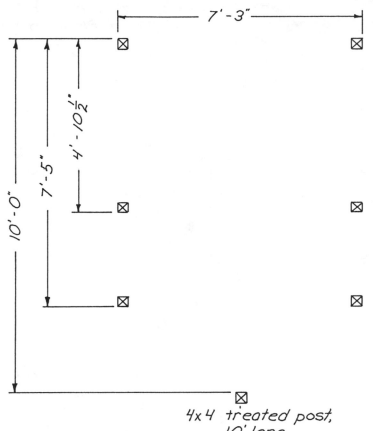

7'-3"

10'-0"

7'-5"

4'-10½"

* Set all posts
  in concrete.

Six 4x4 posts, treated,
8' long.
Set 2' into ground.

* The tops of the
  back six posts
  should be level.
  The front center
  post will be 2'
  higher.

4x4 treated post,
10' long
set 2' into ground.

DETAIL OF NOTCHED TIMBER

Use circular saw with blade
set at angle to make end cuts,
then chisel out notch.

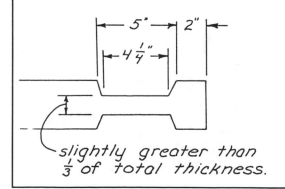

5"   2"

4¼"

slightly greater than
⅓ of total thickness.

* Front and back of play house
  require eleven landscape
  timbers each. Top timber
  and bottom timber should be
  notched on one side only.

Sides of play house require
ten timbers each, plus a
2x4 spacer at top & bottom.

FLOOR JOISTS

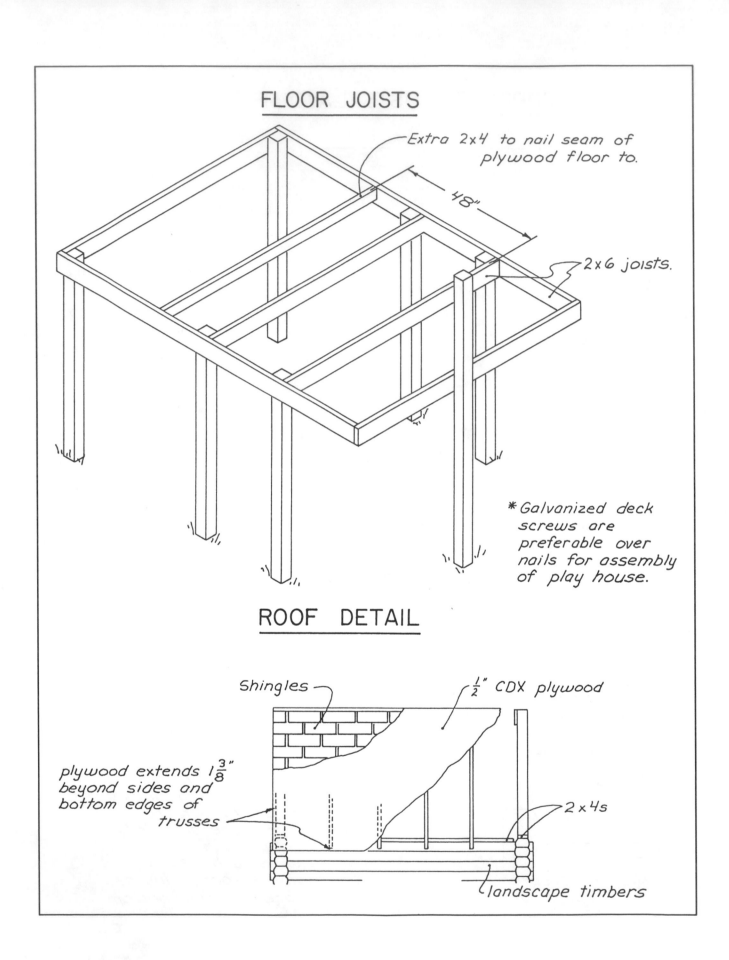

Extra 2x4 to nail seam of plywood floor to.

48"

2x6 joists.

* Galvanized deck screws are preferable over nails for assembly of play house.

ROOF DETAIL

Shingles

$\frac{1}{2}$" CDX plywood

plywood extends $1\frac{3}{8}$" beyond sides and bottom edges of trusses

2 x 4s

landscape timbers

DECK & RAILING

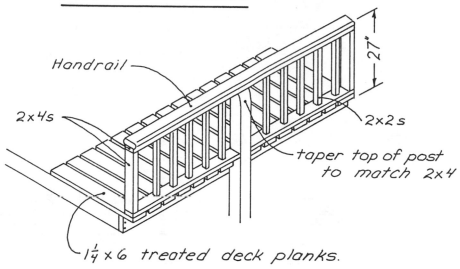

Handrail

2x4s

2x2s

taper top of post to match 2x4

27"

1¼ x 6 treated deck planks.

SANDBOX

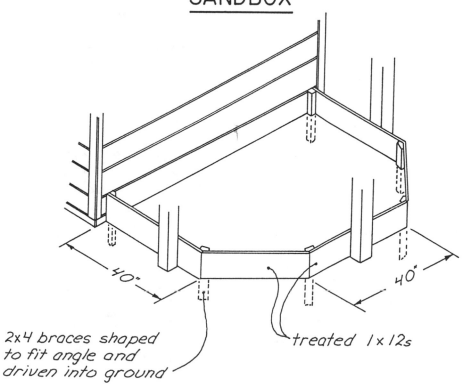

40"

40"

2x4 braces shaped to fit angle and driven into ground

treated 1 x 12s

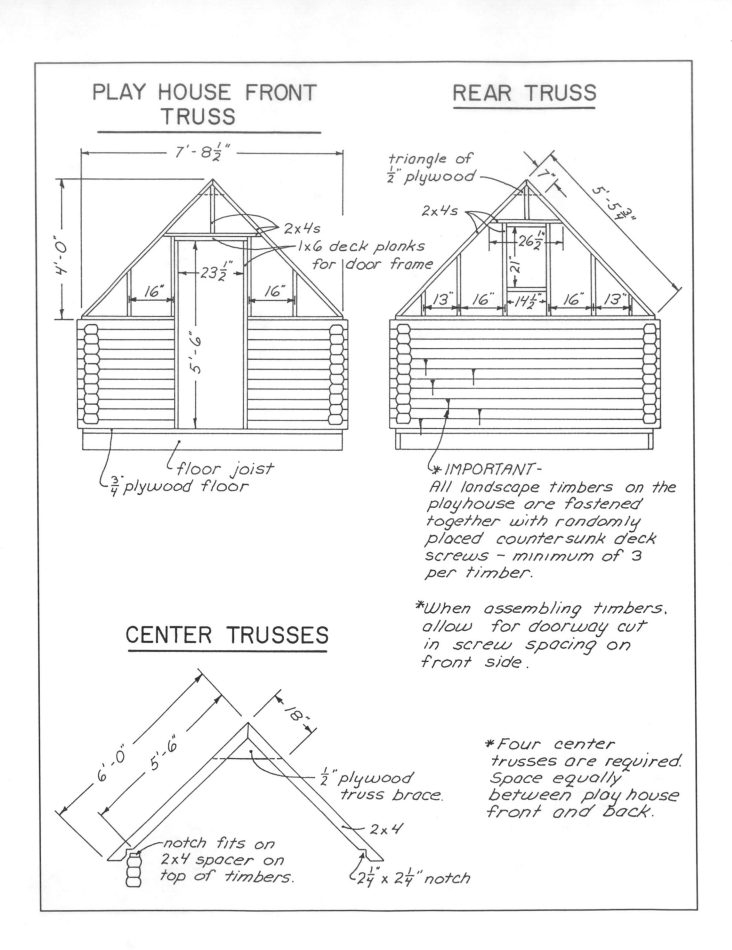

PLAY HOUSE FRONT TRUSS

7'-8½"

4'-0"

2x4s

1x6 deck planks for door frame

23½"

16"   16"

5'-6"

floor joist

¾" plywood floor

REAR TRUSS

triangle of ½" plywood

7"

5'-5¾"

2x4s

26½"

21"

13" 16" 14½" 16" 13"

*IMPORTANT-
All landscape timbers on the playhouse are fastened together with randomly placed countersunk deck screws - minimum of 3 per timber.

*When assembling timbers, allow for doorway cut in screw spacing on front side.

CENTER TRUSSES

18"

6'-0"   5'-6"

½" plywood truss brace.

2x4

notch fits on 2x4 spacer on top of timbers.

2¼" x 2¼" notch

*Four center trusses are required. Space equally between play house front and back.

STORAGE SHED STUD DETAIL

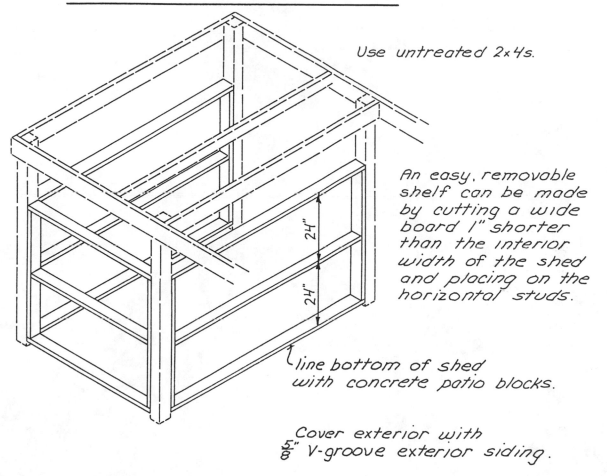

Use untreated 2x4s.

An easy, removable shelf can be made by cutting a wide board 1" shorter than the interior width of the shed and placing on the horizontal studs.

24"

24"

line bottom of shed with concrete patio blocks.

Cover exterior with $\frac{5}{8}$" V-groove exterior siding.

SHED DOOR

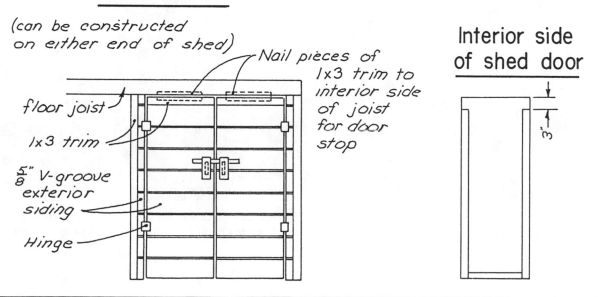

(can be constructed on either end of shed)

Nail pieces of 1x3 trim to interior side of joist for door stop

floor joist

1x3 trim

$\frac{5}{8}$" V-groove exterior siding

Hinge

Interior side of shed door

3"

This version of the Combination Log Cabin Play House/Storage Shed includes stairs with a landing and railing, a bubble window in the roof, and a 2-inch metal pipe attached with a pipe flange.

PVC PIPE PLAY HOUSE

This portable PVC Pipe Play House with matching table and chairs provides a semi-private spot for a game of chess on a lazy summer afternoon.

This versatile little play house complete with a table and two chairs was built for under $100. It is lightweight and portable for moving around the yard for mowing or from one home to the next for those families on the go. Children can use it as a stage for performing plays or holding neighborhood pet shows. Modify the covering and it becomes a stable for a nativity scene. Need to construct a games booth for a children's club or organization? This fits the bill in style!

This play house never needs painting and doesn't rust or rot. It is sturdy enough to withstand rain and wind, and at 5 feet tall it will also fit in your basement. By using screws instead of PVC cement to attach the side and top lengths of pipe to the front and rear panels, the play house can be stored flat when not in use.

WARNING: Because this play house is so lightweight, you *must* anchor it to the ground in some way when it is being used outdoors, so that the wind will not catch it and overturn it and possibly hurt someone. This can be done in various ways, such as tying twine to the bottom joints, holding them firmly to the ground with tent stakes. DO NOT ALLOW CHILDREN NEAR THIS PLAY HOUSE UNLESS IT IS FIRMLY ANCHORED WHEN OUTDOORS.

Required Materials

	Rear Panel	Top & Sides	Front Panel	Table	Two Chairs	TOTAL
Pipe, 1½"			4		8	12
Pipe, 2"	4				8	12
Pipe, 3"	3					3
Pipe, 4"			2			2
Pipe, 6¼"			2			2
Pipe, 7"				4	8	12
Pipe, 11"				4		4
Pipe, 12"					4	4
Pipe, 19¼"			2			2
Pipe, 20¾"			2			2
Pipe, 25"				2		2
Pipe, 30"			2	2		4
Pipe, 34¾"		6				6
Pipe, 38"		2				2
Pipe, 40"			2			2
Pipe, 41"			2			2
Pipe, 60"	2					2
Pipe, 62"	5					5

(Total of 13 lengths of ¾" pipe, 10' long)

	Rear Panel	Top & Sides	Front Panel	Table	Two Chairs	TOTAL
End caps	3	2	4		8	17
Cross	1					1
Outlets	2		2			4
Adapters	2		2			4
Tees	10		9	4	16	39
45° elbows		4				4
90° elbows				4	8	12
Pipe clips				4	8	12

¾" plywood or 1" plywood — one piece 31" x 28½" and two pieces 14" x 10½"
10 yards 45" wide striped fabric
4 yards 45" wide polka dot fabric
16 ¾" round hook-and-loop fasteners
1 can PVC cement
2 cans PVC cleaner

Instructions

PIPE

1 Remove manufacturer's printing from the ¾" pipe with PVC cleaner.

2 Cut pipe to required lengths (see Required Materials), using a plastic tube cutter or a hacksaw in a miter box. Remove any burrs from cut ends with medium-grit sandpaper.

3 Preassemble pipe and fittings according to drawings, *without cement* to be sure everything fits properly. Reassemble *with* cement following directions on back of cement can.

NOTE: This play house can be stored flat when not in use by using wing screws instead of cement to fasten the 60-inch and 62-inch lengths of pipe to the front and rear panels. To do this, after the front and rear panels have been permanently assembled with cement, insert the top and side lengths of pipe in place without cement. Drill small holes through these fitting and pipe joints (only to center, not through the other side) and insert wing screws. To make lining up these holes easier the next time the play house is assembled, draw a line across both the fitting and the pipe and label with a permanent marker (A—A, B—B . . .). You need only label and line the screw joints on the rear panel; the front holes will automatically line up if the rear ones are lined up.

WOOD TOPS

1 Scraps left over from another project work great for the table top and seats. Cut out to required size, rounding off the corners. Sand all surfaces smooth. Paint to match colors in fabric. (The table in the photographs has a green and white checkerboard pattern painted in the center of the table, and a scalloped green border painted around the edges. The chair seats are also painted with green and white checkerboards.) A coat of clear exterior finish can be added for protection against the weather and crayon marks.

2 Attach top and seats to the table and chairs (which have already been assembled with cement) using pipe clips and screws.

FABRIC

1 A variety of fabrics can be used. The stripes-and-polka-dot combination is a natural for kids. Or you may have some old tablecloths, sheets, or tarps that you want to use. Cut out fabric as shown in Fabric Layout diagram.

2 The "A" pieces form the two sides. For each side, sew together selvage edges of two "A" pieces for a center seam. With an iron, press under a 1-inch hem along all four sides;

press under 1 inch again to make a double thickness 1-inch hem. Topstitch $1/8$ inch and $7/8$ inch from the edge.

3 Repeat Step 2 with the "B" pieces for the back.

4 Repeat Step 2 with the "E" pieces for the top.

5 Match up sets of "C" pieces so that the stripes will be running up and down on the two finished triangles. With right sides together, sew two triangle pieces together, leaving an opening to turn it inside out. Turn right side out and press with an iron. Topstitch $1/8$ inch and $7/8$ inch from edges.

6 Sew together strips of "F" pieces to total 210 inches (same as "D" piece). Press seams flat. Put right sides of "D" and "F" pieces together and sew ends and scalloped edge. Turn right side out and press. Fold inside 1 inch of the top edge on both pieces of fabric, and press with iron. Sew top edge $1/8$ inch from edge and $7/8$ inch from edge. Topstitch along scalloped edge.

7 Insert eyelet into each corner and at the center seam of the top, side, and back rectangles. Also insert an eyelet in the center of the hem on the short sides of the top rectangle, and at each point on the triangles.

8 Using sturdy twine, tie these pieces in their proper places on the play house. There should be gaps between the fabric and the pipe for the wind to blow through.

9 Using a cyanoacrylate-type glue (Super Glue™), attach the Velcro® fasteners along the top pipes and fittings of the play house. The scalloped border does not cover the rear of the play house, so have a friend help you hold the border in place to see where the last fastener on each side should be glued. Once the glue has dried, hold the border in place and glue or sew the other side of the fastener to the top edge of the fabric.

FRONT PANEL (exterior side)

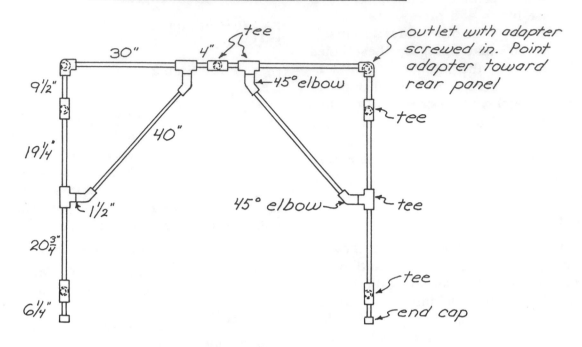

REAR PANEL (interior side)

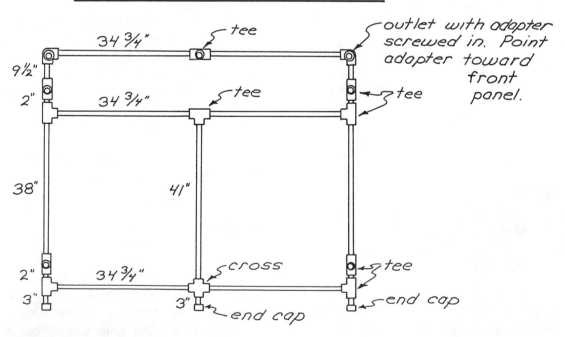

Front and rear panels are connected with two 60" lengths of pipe (insert between adapters) and five 62" lengths of pipe.

TABLE

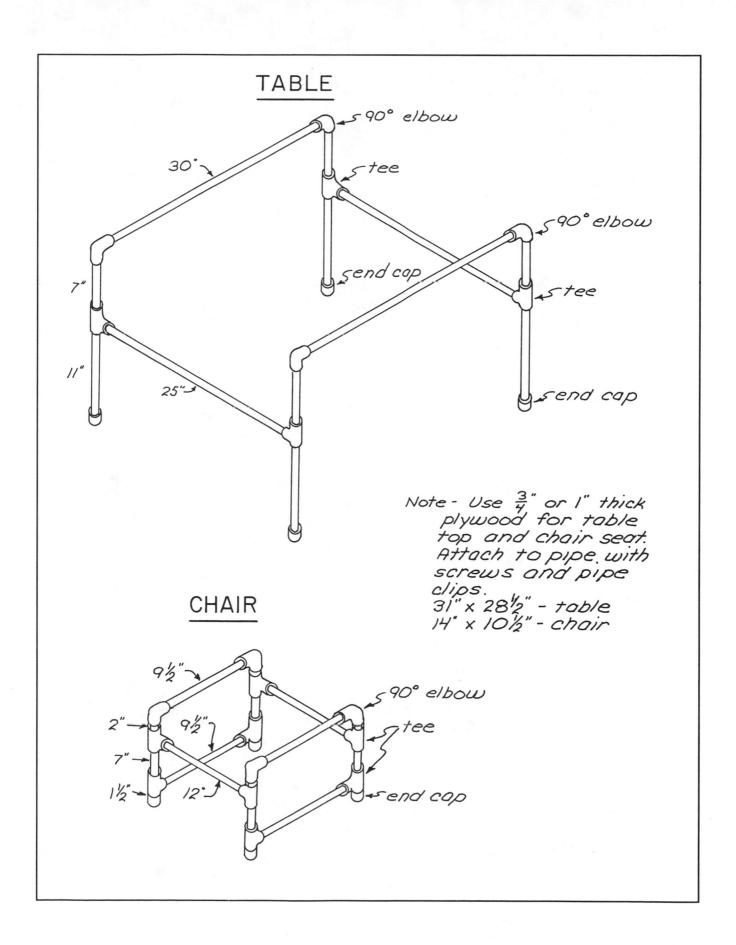

90° elbow

tee

90° elbow

30"

end cap

tee

7"

11"

25"

end cap

Note - Use $\frac{3}{4}$" or 1" thick plywood for table top and chair seat. Attach to pipe. with screws and pipe clips.
31" x 28$\frac{1}{2}$" - table
14" x 10$\frac{1}{2}$" - chair

CHAIR

9$\frac{1}{2}$"

90° elbow

2"

9$\frac{1}{2}$"

tee

7"

1$\frac{1}{2}$"

12"

end cap

FABRIC LAYOUT

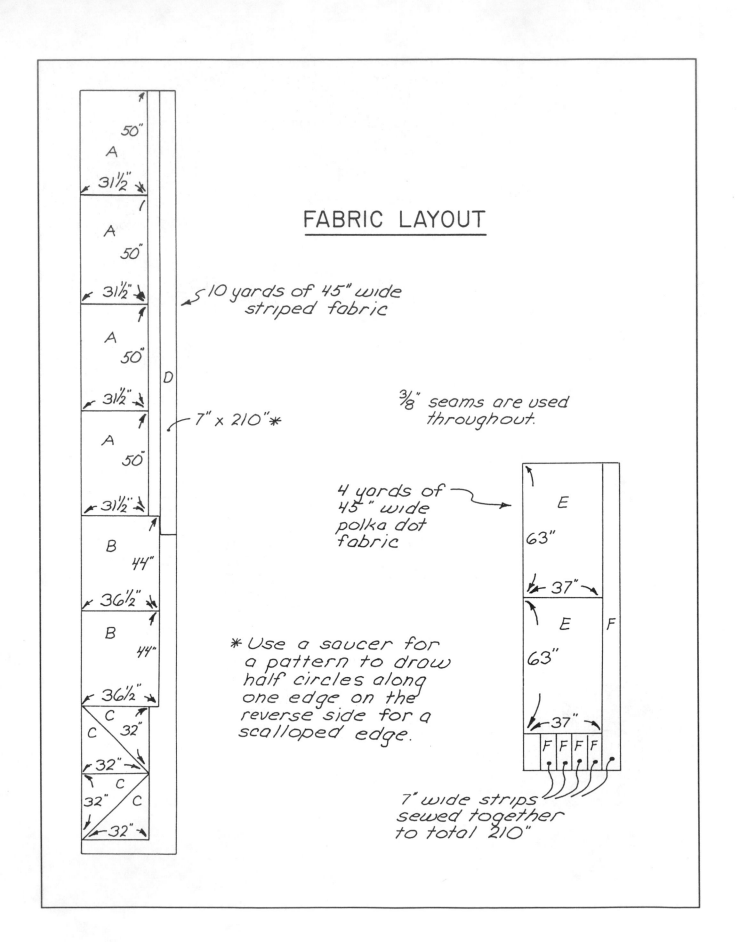

50"

A

31½"

A

50"

31½"

A

50"

D

31½"

A

50"

31½"

B

44"

36½"

B

44"

36½"

C

C   32"

32"

C

32"   C

32"

↙ 10 yards of 45" wide
striped fabric

7" x 210" *

⅜" seams are used
throughout.

4 yards of
45" wide
polka dot
fabric

E

63"

37"

E

63"

F

F F F F

* Use a saucer for
a pattern to draw
half circles along
one edge on the
reverse side for a
scalloped edge.

7" wide strips
sewed together
to total 210"

The PVC Pipe Play House canopy makes a moveable shade for the baby while letting the breeze flow through.

While Mom has a garage sale, the children turn this play house into a profitable concession stand.

JUNGLE PLAY HOUSE

Preschoolers will spend hours in this Jungle Play House, peeping through the holes and hiding toys among the green palm leaves on top.

BROWN FABRIC LAYOUT

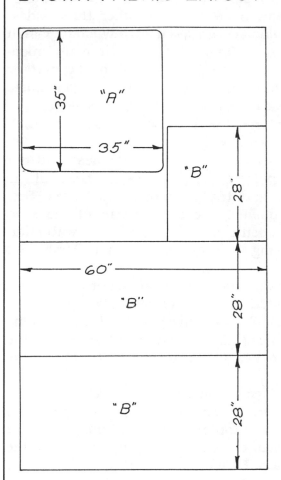

LEAF PATTERN
1 SQUARE = 1 INCH

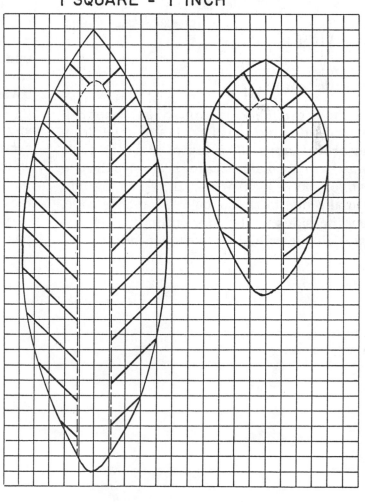

Required Materials

60" wide light brown fabric — 3 yards (Corduroy works great, or use any other sturdy fabric that is heavy enough to hang smoothly)

72" wide green felt—2½ yards

Brown single fold bias tape—2 packages

Stuffing—approximately 2 pounds

Large empty oatmeal box

Brown thread

Green thread

Safety pins

Card table (Instructions given here are for a 34" square card table, 26" high, but they can easily be modified for other sizes and shapes of card tables)

Instructions

Use the Brown Fabric Layout diagram for cutting out sides and top of card table cover from the brown fabric. The top of the card table (plus ½ inch on all sides for seams) is the pattern for piece "A". Sew the "B" pieces together to make one long rectangle 28 inches wide. Sew the sides to the top, cutting off any excess side material, to make a five-sided cube.

Ease cover onto the card table. With a felt marker, draw freehand a door opening on one side and a total of four oval peepholes randomly spaced on the other three sides. These should be drawn slightly smaller than the desired finished size. Cut out the openings, being sure to cut off all of the marker line. Finish off these edges with brown single fold bias tape, and hem the bottom edge.

Enlarge the leaf pattern so that each square equals 1 inch. With the green felt folded in half for double thickness, cut out seven pairs of large leaves (fourteen single leaves) and ten pairs of small leaves. Sew along dashed line of each pair of leaves to make a center rib. Stuff center rib with stuffing, using a dowel to help pack firmly. Set aside.

Cover a large oatmeal box or one of similar height with leftover brown fabric. Glue or hand stitch to attach securely. Use safety pins underneath the brown cover to attach the covered box to the center of the top of the cover.

Put cover on card table. With a needle and green thread, tack the seven large leaves around the top of the covered box. Tack one small leaf on each of the four corners of the table top. Finish the play house by attaching the remaining small leaves to the oatmeal box — on top of the large leaves — for a bushy, palm tree look.

CHILD'S TEPEE

This very inexpensive tepee is small enough to fit into a bedroom or playroom and large enough for little ones to take naps in.

PEGBOARD LAYOUT

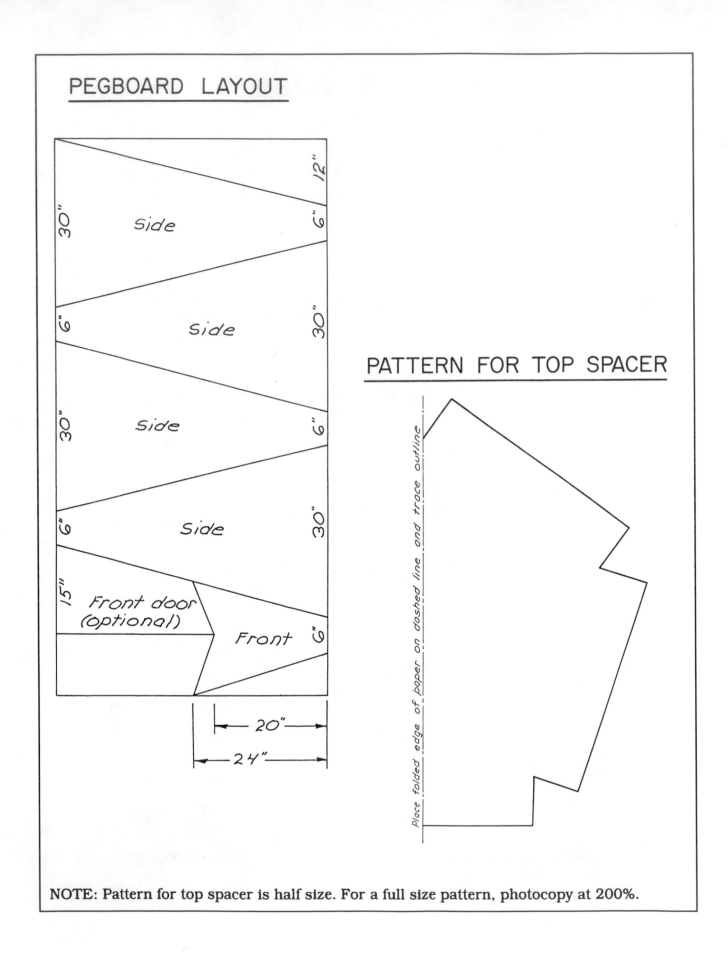

PATTERN FOR TOP SPACER

Side

Side

Side

Side

Front door (optional)

Front

30"   6" | 12"

6"   6"

30"   30"

30"   6"

6"   30"

15"   6"

20"

24"

Place folded edge of paper on dashed line and trace outline

NOTE: Pattern for top spacer is half size. For a full size pattern, photocopy at 200%.

Required Materials

One 4 foot by 8 foot sheet of $1/8$-inch pegboard

Shoelaces or sturdy twine

Five $1/2$-inch dowel rods, 3 feet long

Bright paint

Instructions

1 Cut pegboard as shown in Pegboard Layout diagram. Cut one Top Spacer from one of the scrap pieces of pegboard, using the full-size pattern. This piece is positioned at the top of the sides (on the inside) to make the tepee more rigid.

2 Assemble, using photograph as a guide and tying with the shoelaces or twine in at least three places between each two side panels. Drill one hole (the same size as the pegboard holes) about 6 inches from one end of each dowel rod. When tying together the top corners of the sides, the twine should also go through this hole to keep children from pulling down these rods. Then tie all five dowel rods together at their intersection above the tepee.

3 From inside the tepee, push the top spacer up into position. Tie it to the middle of the top of each of the five sides.

The half door gives the child a little more privacy inside but makes the inside a little darker. Its use is optional.

4 Complete the tepee by painting a few designs on the outside with bright paint (yellow sun, brown arrow, red zigzag border, etc.). You might want to supply the children with various lengths of brightly colored twine. These can be laced again and again through the holes of the pegboard to make additional designs on the sides while improving their eye-hand coordination.

5 Remove all the ties for easy, flat storage under a bed or against the back wall of a closet.

IMPORTANT: Use double knots on all ties to prevent children from accidentally undoing the knots and collapsing the tepee.

8'x8' PLAY HOUSE

This scale model play house was finished to resemble the old play house in the photograph on page 46.

There is something enormously satisfying about constructing a building from the ground up. This play house offers a great opportunity to test your carpentry skills and creativity. The simple square design is as basic as possible. If you have never attempted to construct a frame building before, check out a good, illustrated basic carpentry book from the library and read up on safe construction methods. Use it as a guide as you come to details such as how to trim a door opening and install the door, or how to enclose the overhang if desired. Take your time and enjoy the knowledge and experience you are accumulating.

Be sure to check your local code requirements and obtain a building permit if required. If you are uncomfortable with using general guidelines such as those given here, there is a variety of detailed step-by-step play house plans available at hardware stores and lumber yards. The plans given here are general and flexible in order to accommodate building materials already on hand and individual tastes.

Windows and doors are expensive, so if you are trying to build a play house as inexpensively as possible, it's a good idea to obtain these items first and work the rest of the design around them. Look for bargains at lumber yards and garage sales. If you notice a house that is undergoing extensive remodeling, ask the owner if there are any windows he or she plans to throw out.

Once you know the sizes of the windows and door that you will be using, be sure to space the 2 x 4 wall studs to accommodate them. Keep the center stud in the center so that two sheets of plywood, siding, or paneling will fit nicely on each side of the structure.

Make certain all corners of the concrete slab are square. Use 2-inch lumber to build the forms for it and brace securely. Don't underestimate the pushing power of wet concrete. Take your time and be sure this slab is exactly 8 feet by 8 feet and exactly square.

All wood that will be exposed to the weather in the finished play house should be treated lumber. The 2 x 4s that are bolted onto the concrete slab should also be treated lumber.

For many people the most difficult part of constructing a building is constructing the rafters. Since the concrete slab is exactly 8 feet wide (same as the top 2 x 4s), why not construct the rafters on the slab before framing the walls? They will be easier to work with at ground level. Cut one out, nail together, and check for fit on the concrete. Use it as a pattern to cut the rest. After the wall framing is completed, the rafters can be lifted up into place.

Use your imagination in deciding how to finish the interior and exterior of the play house. Siding can be applied horizontally, vertically, at an angle, or at a double angle. Make it Victorian or contemporary; add a front porch or a little rear patio. Finish off the interior with paneling or wallpaper, leave it unfinished, or assign that part of the project to the child. Most important of all: make it safe and make it fun.

NOTE: Either you or your child (if old enough) might want to make a scale model of your proposed play house before building the actual one, particularly if you have never constructed a building before. A 1" = 1' scale is a good workable size. Use balsa wood available at hobby stores for scale size lumber and plywood, and cut up sandpaper for shingles. It's a great wintertime project, and the finished model is sure to become a family keepsake.

Making a scale model of the frame of a proposed play house is good practice—and fun!

FRONT FRAMING

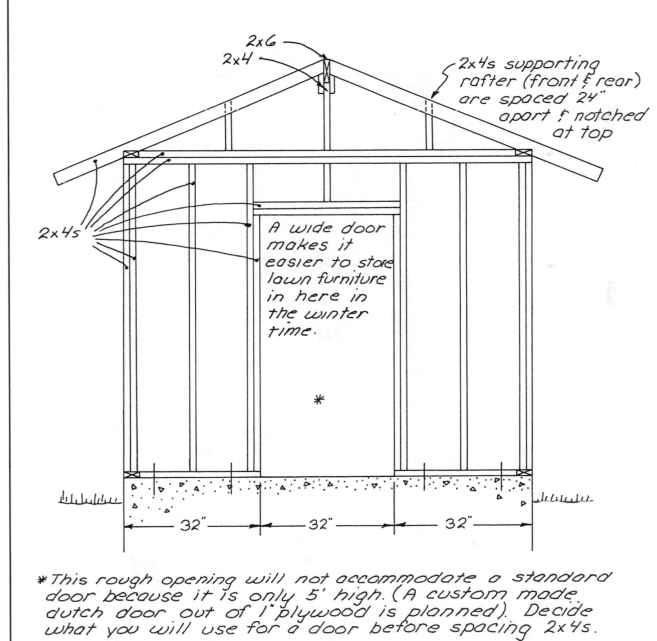

2x6

2x4

2x4s supporting rafter (front & rear) are spaced 24" apart & notched at top

2x4s

A wide door makes it easier to store lawn furniture in here in the winter time.

*

32"   32"   32"

*This rough opening will not accommodate a standard door because it is only 5' high. (A custom made dutch door out of 1" plywood is planned). Decide what you will use for a door before spacing 2x4s.

LEFT & RIGHT SIDE FRAMING

the 2x6 ridge board and the top 2x4 on each side extend out 1'-0" to support overhang rafter.

rafter ties

Windows are expensive, so find a good buy on two (one for each side) and adjust the rough opening size here. This one is for a double casement window.

24" 24" 24" 24"

use treated lumber for bottom 2x4s

1/2" x 10" anchor bolt (total of 13 used). Set 1¾" from edge in wet concrete with at least 2½" above concrete surface. (Hint: drill required holes in bottom 2x4s and use as a template to check placement of bolts while concrete is still wet.)

REAR FRAMING

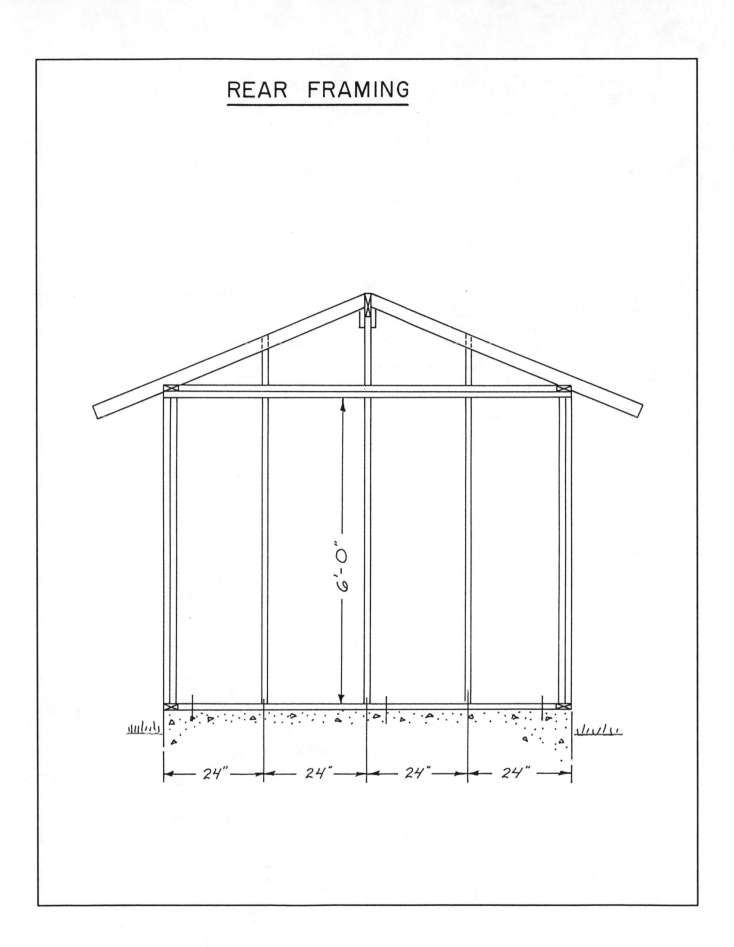

CENTER SECTION AT A RAFTER

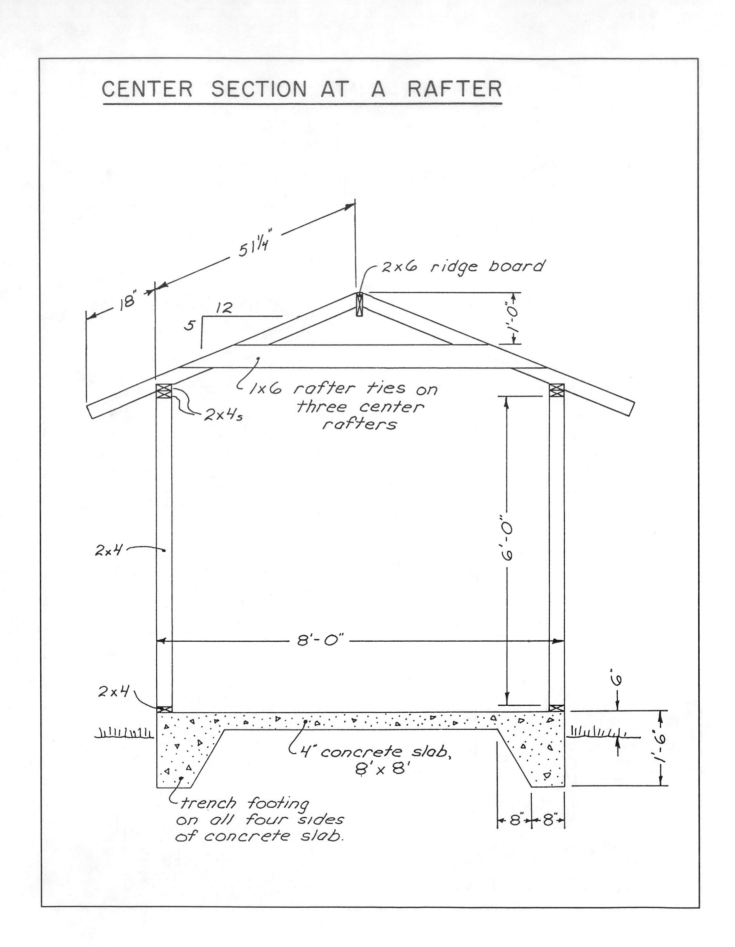

51¼"

18"

5 / 12

2x6 ridge board

1'-0"

1x6 rafter ties on three center rafters

2x4s

2x4

6'-0"

8'-0"

2x4

6"

1'-6"

4" concrete slab, 8' x 8'

trench footing on all four sides of concrete slab.

8" 8"

SAMPLE 8' x 8' PLAY HOUSE FRONTS

Amy's Cottage

Davis School

Jaime Davis, teacher

design your own

Scottsville RR Depot

PLAY CASTLE

(Provided by the American Plywood Association, designed by John Underbrink.)

Play Castle. Courtesy of American Plywood Association, Tacoma, Washington.

Panel Layouts
Five 3/4" x 4' x 8' APA Trademarked Panels

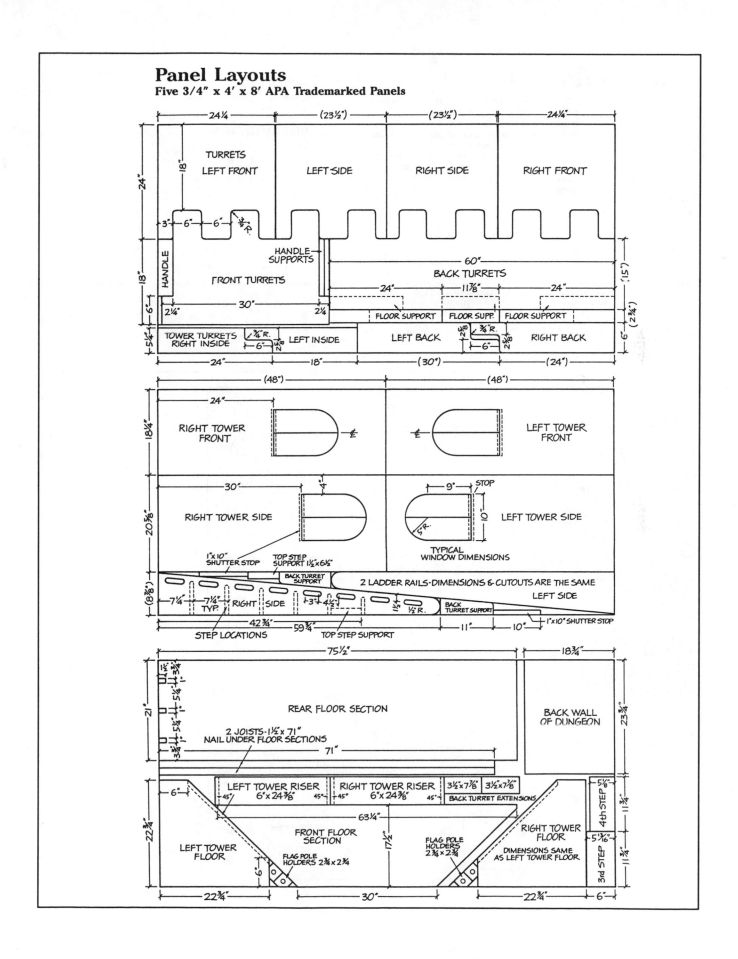

Materials List

Recommended panels: APA trademarked Medium Density Overlay (MDO), overlaid both sides, APA trademarked A-B or A-C, or APA trademarked nonveneer structural wood panels such as waferboard or oriented strand board. In the model castle pictured, APA waferboard panels were used on the castle front to give a textured finish. MDO panels were used in other sections of the castle.

Project Notes: Draw pattern on panels as shown. Because of the large number of pieces, label all sections before cutting. Before assembly, round all corners and edges with a 1/4 in. bullnose router bit. Castle can be assembled in four sections: the front turret walls, drawbridge, and front half of platform; left side and ladder; back turret and rear platform; and right side and slide/dungeon. When all four sections are complete, castle can be finished and assembled in desired location. The four sections should be bolted together for optimum stability. To finish the castle, use your choice of paints or stains. In the model pictured, decorative bricks were cut in half and glued to the turret walls.

This plan was a winner in the Panel Project Contest sponsored by the American Plywood Association and *Popular Science* magazine.

Designed by **John M. Underbrink, Kirkland, Washington.**

PANELS

Quantity	Description
5	3/4 in. x 4 ft. x 8 ft.

OTHER MATERIALS

Quantity	Description
1	8 ft. x 1 in. dowel
11 sets	3 in. T-hinges
300	Wood screws
8	3/8 in. x 1-1/2 in. hex bolts
2	3/8 in. x 2 - 2-1/2 in. hex bolts
10	Washers
10	T-nuts (blind nuts)
2	1 x 3 lumber strips, in 10 in. lengths
2	Flagpoles (4 ft. x 1 in. each)
4	Screw-in eye hooks — 2 open, 2 closed
1	7 ft. black plastic chain
As required	Wood glue, paint, decorative brick

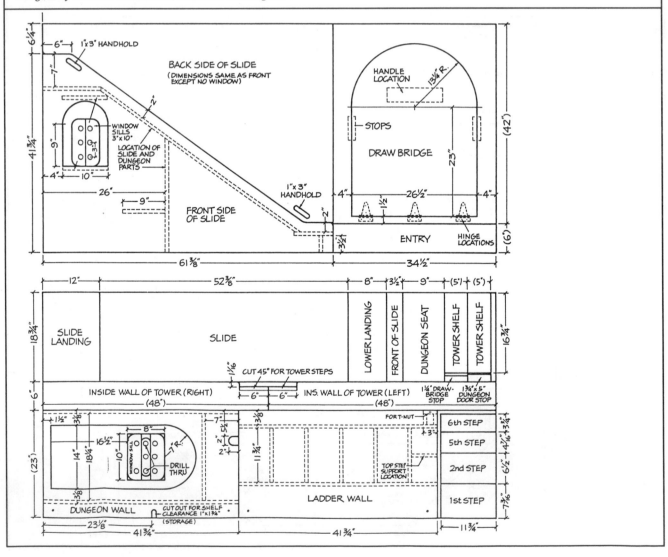

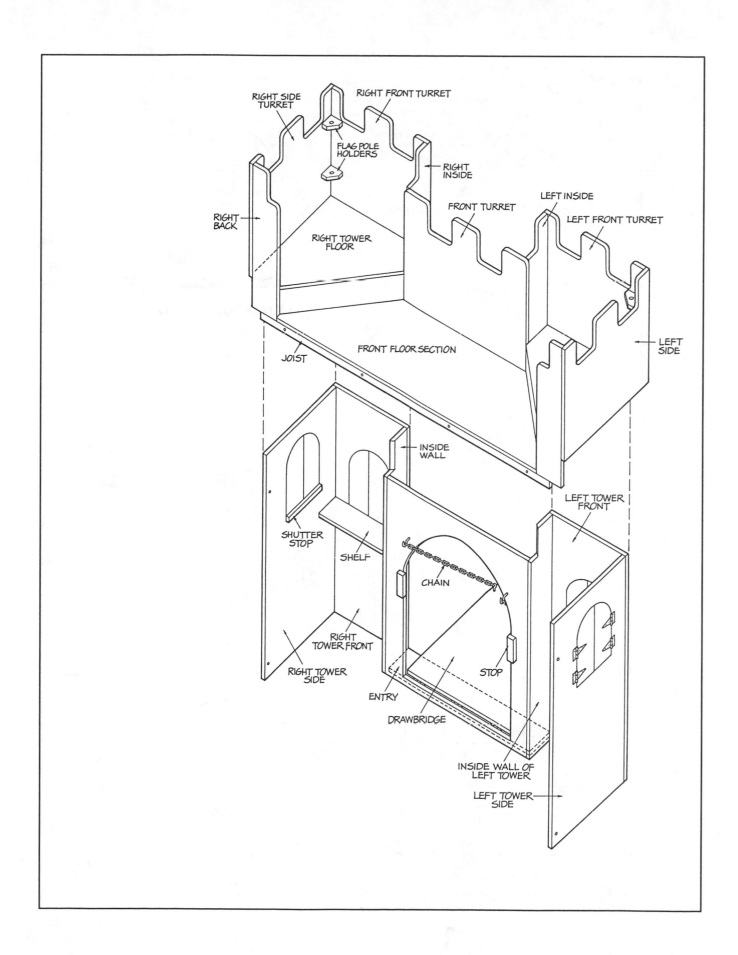

RIGHT SIDE TURRET

RIGHT FRONT TURRET

FLAG POLE HOLDERS

RIGHT INSIDE

FRONT TURRET

LEFT INSIDE

LEFT FRONT TURRET

RIGHT BACK

RIGHT TOWER FLOOR

FRONT FLOOR SECTION

LEFT SIDE

JOIST

INSIDE WALL

LEFT TOWER FRONT

SHUTTER STOP

SHELF

CHAIN

STOP

RIGHT TOWER FRONT

RIGHT TOWER SIDE

ENTRY

DRAWBRIDGE

INSIDE WALL OF LEFT TOWER

LEFT TOWER SIDE

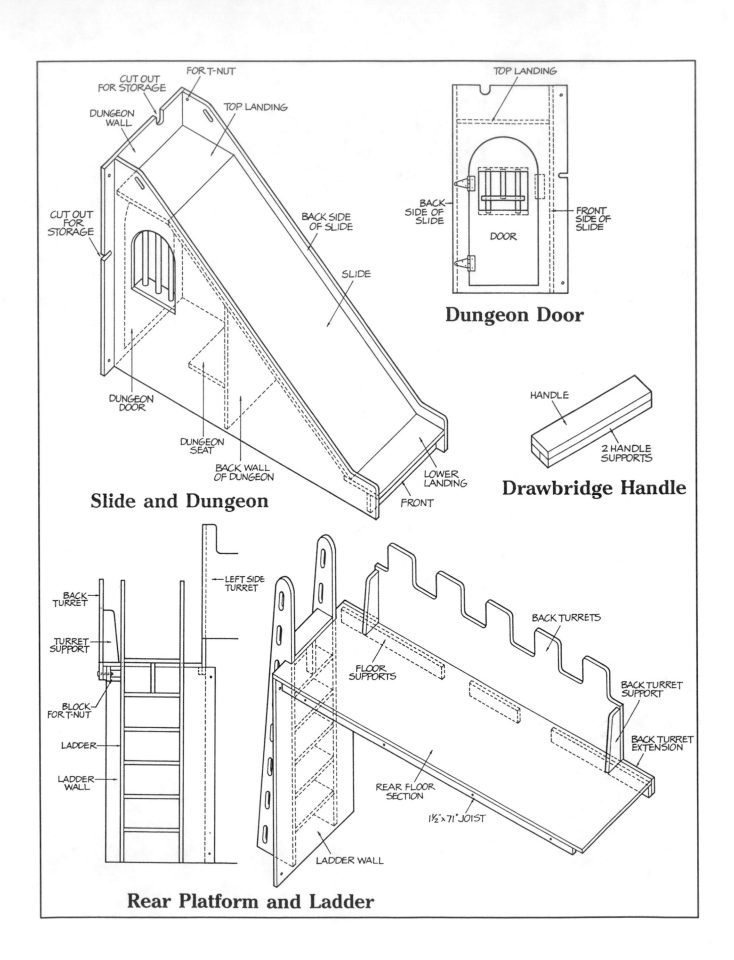

CUT OUT FOR STORAGE

FOR T-NUT

DUNGEON WALL

TOP LANDING

CUT OUT FOR STORAGE

BACK SIDE OF SLIDE

SLIDE

DUNGEON DOOR

DUNGEON SEAT

BACK WALL OF DUNGEON

LOWER LANDING

FRONT

Slide and Dungeon

TOP LANDING

BACK SIDE OF SLIDE

FRONT SIDE OF SLIDE

DOOR

Dungeon Door

HANDLE

2 HANDLE SUPPORTS

Drawbridge Handle

BACK TURRET

TURRET SUPPORT

BLOCK FOR T-NUT

LADDER

LADDER WALL

LEFT SIDE TURRET

FLOOR SUPPORTS

BACK TURRETS

BACK TURRET SUPPORT

BACK TURRET EXTENSION

REAR FLOOR SECTION

1½"×71" JOIST

LADDER WALL

Rear Platform and Ladder

Afterword

Perhaps browsing through these pages has brought back memories of a special childhood retreat of your own. What was it like? Are you of the generation that knows what yelling "Pigtail" means when playing Andy-Over, or are you more familiar with the computer-zapping generation? What kinds of furnishings were in your play house? Where was it located? What eventually happened to it?

Have you designed a play house for your child? Does it sit in the lofty heights of a tree, make use of recycled materials, or have unusual components? Is the design conservative, wild, a replica of some other structure, or a wonderful hodgepodge of scavenged parts? What makes it uniquely yours?

I have already begun collecting material for Book No. 2 on American play houses and tree houses—past and present. I invite you to write and share your experiences.

Kathy Smith Anthenat
Play House Memories
10016 Crow's Nest Cove
Reminderville, OH 44202

Index